Praise for *A Hero in a Bandana*

Luke Gregory, CEO, Monroe Carell Jr. Children's Hospital at Vanderbilt:

"The poignant words and actions of Dr. Hoover and his family serve as heartfelt reminders for all of us in who work in healthcare of the special honor and privilege we have to serve patients. The Hoovers have further committed themselves to improve the lives of future generations of patients through their research, medical practice and tireless fundraising. Brad and Michelle are devoted to their family and to their faith and values. They are true heroes."

Gordon Kennedy, quintessential Nashville musician, producer, and 2-time Grammy winner songwriter ("Change The World", 1997 Song of the Year recorded by Eric Clapton):

"There's a sentiment that God dropped into my heart recently that I use to describe stories like this - It breaks the heart and then puts it back together again, stronger than it was before, and it does this all at once."

Neil Thrasher, Nashville artist and A-list songwriter for Rascal Flatts, Kenny Chesney, Jason Aldean, others:

"What a privilege it has been to play a small part in Brad and Michelle's own "Walk Through The Valley". Their strength, courage and perseverance is an inspiration to all who know them."

A Hero in a Bandana

A Family's Walk Through the Valley

Brad W. Hoover, MD

Cover design: James Kelley, Reverse Creative

ISBN: 978-0-9911915-4-3

Published by Brad W. Hoover

Printed in the United States of America

Contents

Foreword

In the spring of 2006 two of our grandsons were confirmed at Holy Family Catholic Church in Brentwood, Tennessee. It is customary, in the Catholic tradition, for those being confirmed to take a new name. Most choose Saints whom they respect and would like to emulate. Others choose names of individuals whom they admire, respect, and wish to honor. There were over 150 eighth graders in the class, so the ceremony was long. Never-the-less, I was able to stay alert enough to notice that many of the boys were taking the name "Liam". I had not heard of St. Liam, but realized that there are thousands of saints and I was not blessed to know all of them.

After the ceremony I asked my daughter-in-law, Janet, whose son was in the confirmation class, about St. Liam whose name so many of the boys were using. She informed me he was the late son of Brad Hoover, one of her partners. I recalled she had told me some time before that Brad's son had died of a brain tumor but I had not met either Brad or his son, Liam. She went on to tell me of Liam's struggle to live and how much he was admired by all those who knew him.

I wondered how on earth his parents, Brad and Michelle, ever survived this tragedy. I wonder that about all parents who face such seemingly unstoppable pain.

As a pediatrician I have seen too many kids die, not a lot, but any is too many. In pediatrics every death is seen as a failure. I feel this failure every time a child dies, even kids I don't know or never treated. I have never been able to overcome that feeling of hopelessness; it is a feeling which makes me uncomfortable meeting the grieving parents.

Not long after Liam's death I met Brad and Michelle, at Janet's and my son Sean's, Christmas open house. As much as I wanted to meet Brad as a colleague, I didn't know what to say to him and Michelle. I, like so many others, am not good with words at a time like this. Janet made the introduction and I was able to mouth my condolences for the loss of their son without my voice cracking.

I was happy the dim light prevented them from seeing the tears in my eyes. "Thank you," Michelle replied. "We'll never get over his death, but we have learned to get through it and on with our lives." Then she introduced me to the toddler Brad was holding in his arms and told me how lucky they were that God had sent a beautiful baby for them to adopt! Somehow the grieving parents often make it easier for us.

Later Brad and I went to Haiti on a medical mission with Janet and other members of our church. There I began to know Brad and appreciate his faith, his medical knowledge, and his compassion. Sometime later he asked me to write the foreword for *A Hero in a Bandana*. I am honored.

To say that Brad is an emergency care physician would be true, but it is more complete to say Brad is a father and a husband. *Hero in A Bandana* is the story of how he and his family navigated their son's fight with brain cancer, their son's death, and how they managed the pain.

I can't imagine what it must be like to go through what they experienced! I only know how I felt after my puppy died some 15 years ago. What I felt was a wrist burn from a pizza pan, they faced Hiroshima.

A Hero in A Bandana is taken from the journal Brad wrote during his son's illness and is filled with all the emotion - hope, love, disappointment, and more, that we can only imagine. But woven through it all was his pride in how Liam behaved and accepted his illness. This pride supported Brad and Michelle during those devastating times. Frequently desperate, he never despaired.

Interspersed in the journal Brad adds commentary gathered from his life strengthening resolve to be a better man, see good come from suffering, and to do all he can to support research into prevention and treatment of childhood cancer.

Throughout the story Brad shares his faith and finds solace in prayer and in the music that has filled his life and that of his family. In the middle of all this pain and anguish, Dr. Hoover quotes an article from *Readers Digest*: "*...prayer is ultimately about realms of consciousness as yet unexplored--about what believers might call the soul, or the spirit, or some transcendent part of being. Some believe that prayers are actually answered. But it doesn't really matter: For those who believe, that is not where the true power of prayer will ever reside.*"

I found the discussion of prayer in the midst of grief, a personal release from grief's grip. It cemented Brad's faith to mine and I felt his connection to our Creator. I know readers will find the context of that discussion to be an aid to their own prayer life.

Near the end of this little book, Dr. Hoover shares a story written for another boy named Liam who died at the age of 5 of a brain tumor. In "The Brave Little Soul", author John Alessi explains why people suffer and how good can come from it. It is one of the best explanation of suffering I have ever seen. I'll not tell you more about it, it is so good you need to read it yourself!

A Hero in a Bandana: A Family's Walk Through the Valley, is short, endearing, inspirational and gripping. I hope and pray that I have done justice to this great little book. And that my words are a tribute to Liam, his strong, compassionate dad, and his family.

As a postscript to Liam's life the Hoovers have established the Hoover Hope Foundation. Through it they have contributed close than $1 million dollars to St. Jude's Hospital, Vanderbilt's Monroe Carroll Children's Hospital, and other groups which help children who have cancer and their families.

The world truly needs more men and women like Michelle and Brad. With Liam watching over them I'm sure his sister and new little brother will become people like their parents. "Thanks God for giving this wonderful family to us. Continue to bless them and those who know them."

Parnell Donahue, M.D.

Author of *Messengers in Denim, Tools for Effective Parenting*, and (coming in 2015) *What Every Dad and Mom, Tween and Teen Need to Know about Sex.*

Preface

I began this email journal of a parent's worse dream realized, before Facebook became popular and outside of the social-sharing sites such as CaringBridge, as a way of keeping our circle of family and close friends informed of just what was happening to Liam and to us. These emails are in italics throughout the book, in original form. The regular font style represent my supplements for the purpose of bridging these various updates into a manuscript. I had no intention of publishing, but was encouraged along the way to consider doing so; if nothing else than to provide insight and/or help for a future family walking this path. I met with a couple of marketing friends who made suggestions, had a English teacher associate at my wife's school provide expert editing, and added a few pictures. I may have submitted a book proposal a time or two, and met with a literary agent and emailed a few more. Each time, the answer was thanks but no thanks.

Which was fine with me, and the manuscript literally sat on the shelf (or, in a drawer). I thought one day something may come of it, and the timing would be as Solomon so adequately put it in Ecclesiastes 3:1. In February of 2014, nearly 10 years from the time of Liam's diagnosis, that time came. The local county library where we resided sponsored a literary award contest for local authors, with the winners in each category were awarded a publishing package. On a whim, I sent my manuscript via Dropbox and went about my day. In May of that year, I was notified I had won the nonfiction category award and the rest, they say, is history.

But it continues. Talk about how one good turn deserves another... I had no clue as to how to begin to design a cover or the technical requirements thereof. Yet, a fellow alumni fraternity brother (KA) who I had yet to meet in person reached out and offered his design company services to do it for me. We 'met' through an email campaign earlier in the year regarding raising funds to purchase a new house for the active fraternity chapter in Martin, Tennessee. I had made a donation, which was shared with the actives and alumni via social media, and this gentleman emailed me that if ever I needed his assistance to please call on him. The cover of my book is the work of his talented, and giving, hand.

All proceeds from this book will benefit the foundation my wife began to assist other families of pediatric cancer patients - Hoover Hope Foundation. We have been able to give back to others through donations to St. Jude Children's Hospital and an endowment created at the Monroe Carell Jr Children's Hospital at Vanderbilt. We have done so through several years of a 5K walk/run, an ever-increasing bicycle ride through the pastoral Middle Tennessee country roads, and several songwriters' nights events at the majestic Franklin Theatre and the legendary Bluebird Cafe. Visit us at www.hooverhope.org. There you find a video embedded on the home page of an interview conducted and produced by Liam's school, featuring Michelle and I along with selected faculty and his classmates. We have a donation link as well, and information on upcoming events.

If you, or someone you know, is traversing a rocky path of cancer or any disease or trauma, perhaps you will see how our family walked the walk, and continue to try and do so. If this book can assist you on that journey, clear a stick on the path or guide you over a stump, then I have succeeded. You are not alone.

Prologue

"Can I send her over to talk with you?"

Every so often, someone you know does something that at the time seems rather trivial, but the result makes a profound change on your and your family's lives forever. One such event occurred for my family in March of 1993. I was a general medical officer in the U.S. Army, stationed near Nuremberg, Germany. My wife Michelle and I were nearing the end of a three-year tour there, which had begun less than a month after our wedding and had included within it a four-and-one-half-month duty to Saudi Arabia and Iraq for me for Operation Desert Shield/Storm. Despite that challenge and others weathered as newlyweds in a foreign land, we had enjoyed our time in Europe.

One portion of our lives though was missing: children. While we had two dogs and a cat, we longed for a baby to add to the mix. After months of testing, we had found that we were unable to conceive naturally. Michelle had endured two surgeries as well, but there would be no changing the physiology. Later, we even gave IVF a go, but to no avail. Adoption then became option #1 for us to become parents. While I had no personal experience with the concept of adoption, Michelle had an adopted sister and rather quickly convinced me that this was our future in to have and raise children.

A fellow officer in my unit and his wife had successfully adopted a girl from Romania a couple of years earlier. In fact, the adoption became final while we were in the midst of Desert Shield (picture his homecoming). Michelle and I had that in the forefront of our minds when we decided to pursue a similar course. One of the civilian physicians in the hospital where I practiced was from Romania and told me she had a colleague in a city there that might be able to help us adopt a child there. When she mentioned a beautiful newborn girl that was available, we made our arrangements to visit and pursue. We flew into Timisoara, a city on the western edge of the country, and met the doctor at his flat. He took us over to the orphanage, and had us wait in the car while he went in to discuss the matter with the personnel there. As our wait in the car lengthened, we had a feeling that things were not going well inside.

When he returned, he confirmed our suspicion by informing us that the director was unwilling to begin any portion of the adoption process, including our even seeing the child, unless an agency was involved [there had been a rash of baby-selling incidents in Romania of late, and agency-assisted adoptions were becoming the norm]. So our journey continued with an eight-hour train trip to the capital, Bucharest, to meet with an adoption agency representative. We met him at a restaurant there, and he provided us with information and paperwork that would be needed to initiate the process of a foreign adoption. It was clear that we would leave Romania without a child, but not without hope for the future.

After our return to Germany, we resigned ourselves to pick up the adoption process once stateside. We thought perhaps to take one last vacation before our return, and Greece would be it! (Still haven't taken that Greece trip).

A few months earlier, Michelle and I had employed a social worker to conduct a home study for us, in anticipation of a foreign adoption. I sent out an intranet message to my colleagues in the OB and family practice departments of the hospital, informing them of our home study and desire to adopt. At the end of the message, I asked them to keep us in mind should they hear of a single mother wanting to pursue adoption. I had almost forgotten that line when I got a call from a family practitioner one day, asking if we were still actively looking to adopt. I told him that we definitely were interested and that we had been disappointed from our Romanian trip. He then said he had a patient about thirty weeks along in pregnancy who had not had any prenatal care. He said that all was well with the pregnancy and that the mother was interested in giving up the child for adoption. She was a single enlisted soldier, with an older child born from wedlock being cared for by her mother in the States and did not want to go that route again. She had had no relationship with the birth father since conception and planned to resume her military career after delivery. She had considered early termination of the pregnancy, but she presented to a clinic too late for that option before her arrival in Germany.

I told him to send the soldier over to the emergency room where I was on duty that day. He did, and I met her and gave her a copy of our home study to peruse. That weekend, Michelle and I invited her for dinner at our home so she could get to know us. The dinner went well, and the following week, she informed her superior officer that she wanted us to adopt her child. She told us later that the home visit had convinced her when she noticed one of our dachshunds with a cast on its leg. The dog had a congenital knee dislocation, and she had undergone surgery recently from a local vet. The soldier remarked that if we could show that much care and concern over a pet, then we would make excellent parents. Naturally, we couldn't have agreed more.

The next few weeks were a flurry of activity, with legal papers to be drawn for all parties to sign and have notarized. William Bond Hoover was born a healthy 9 lbs. and 5 oz. on May 11, 1993. He went home with us two days later. Less than three weeks after that, our tour ended and the three of us arrived in San Antonio for the next phase of our lives. To say we were a bit dizzy from the events of the month preceding our return to the U.S. is quite the understatement. Although with time passages I haven't kept in contact with my family practitioner colleague, I hope that he truly understands the impact he made on our lives with his "referral" that day.

We arrived at our son's name through a combination of influences. William is the formal appellation from which the names of both my father (Bill) and Michelle's father (Billy) are derived. Bond is Michelle's maiden name. We were friends with a family in Germany whose youngest son was named Liam, and we always liked it (and him!). When we discovered that "Liam" was an Irish derivative of "William" (the last four letters) – we had our nickname.

Oh, a post-script from the Romanian adventure. As I alluded, all was not lost from that trip, as I remembered the agency where the social worker worked (located, in all places, in Hermitage, Tennessee, a suburb of Nashville where I now practice). I called the agency in 1995 to inquire about a foreign adoption, mentioning our meeting with the Romanian representative. The agency representative I spoke with was very helpful and advised us to consider Latvia as a place to adopt. They had only recently begun allowing adoptions from there, and he suggested that we should "strike while the iron's hot". We took his sound advice, and eighteen months later (via the formal international adoption process) became the proud parents of a baby girl. Aubrey Danielle, born Daiga Belousa to a deaf-mute mother out of wedlock, was our final stone to the family we had constructed.

We were a complete family, blessed with both a handsome boy and his beautiful sister. Funny, I don't recall Liam ever describing Aubrey in such a term, but he loved his little sister nonetheless. We enjoyed activities together, as varied as beach fun in the summer and snow skiing in the winter. We settled in a suburb of Nashville in early 1998, after my completion of service in the Army in June of that year. Liam was a member of the inaugural first-grade class at an elementary school built two streets from ours, and loved riding his bike there with his friends whenever the weather permitted. Our neighborhood was teeming with youngsters of Liam's and Aubrey's age, and they made acquaintances easily. Liam in particular meshed with Chadwick, whom he met in first grade, and Eric, who came along in third. Those "three amigos" played together almost daily it seems, or at least some combination thereof did. When Brian and Liam became closer friends in the fifth grade, we knew that he would be at one of their houses if he was not at ours.

Liam, while never what you would call a sports enthusiast, nevertheless enjoyed participating in soccer, Little League baseball, and (his favorite) flag football. I was fortunate to be able to coach him in the latter, witnessing his lumbering self make it in the end zone on one memorable Saturday morning. He got more enjoyment though out of a typical neighborhood game of "wall-ball" or "kick the can" with his buddies in the 'hood. Now electronics – that was a separate category of entertainment. Whether hand-held or played via a console, he was quite tech-savvy for his age with a variety of games. Michelle and I always knew that one of our most effective forms of discipline was to restrict him from them.

Vacations in our family were taken in a variety of locales, but Liam's favorite place to be was his first official hometown, San Antonio. The number one reason for that was his Aunt Meg, with whom he shared a very special bond. When we moved to San Antonio when Liam was 3 weeks old, my sister Meg was in the process of relocating back there herself. Her husband was still in the Dallas area, and she needed a temporary weekday residence for a few months until they completed their move. We moved her into our spare bedroom while she worked during the week, and she and Liam began what would be a lifelong connection not unlike a mother-son type. She would spoil him on occasion, but the love she gave to him was what would draw him like a magnet when he would angle to visit there after our move in 1996. She now has three boys of her own, but Liam will always be her "first". She took him along on Florida vacations, and on one day in June 2003 she asked him to call me and leave me a message on my cell phone. I never deleted it – you will see why a little later.

Perhaps our most memorable vacation was one we took in the summer of 2003 to Alaska. I have a high-school classmate who lives in Anchorage, and we anchored our trip from there. Hiking, fishing, swimming, moose-watching, bear-looking, and more were packed into those two weeks; we enjoyed every minute. We knew that we might not be able to ever return to such a place again.

Chapter 1

Headaches

The summer of 2004 began with a celebration. These days, elementary school kids "graduate" into middle school, with some pomp and circumstance mixed in. The real highlight though is the party that follows. At Liam's fifth grade class party in late May, it was a hoot to watch the boys and girls dance (not with each other, of course) to the tunes spun by a DJ. I don't know when I had seen Liam smiling and laughing as much as on that day.

The following week, we embarked for Boy Scout camp in East Tennessee. This was his first experience with camp, having just joined the BSA when he turned 11 in early May. I went along with him and the troop for the week. The first night, the boys were so hyped that sleep was an afterthought to them (and consequently to the adult leaders). So it was no surprise the next day when Liam told me he had a headache. It was nothing major and did not even require a remedy as it was gone within minutes. I do remember his falling down later that day during horseplay and skinning his leg in the process. After getting him cleaned up and applying some first aid, he was all set in that bed for night #2. "Dad," he called out to me as I was departing for my tent, "Thanks for taking care of me."

He mentioned a headache a couple of more times that week, and I probably gave him a single Tylenol each time. I felt that he had plenty of reasons to hurt with the heat, sleep deprivation, and physical exhaustion. It did not slow him down one iota, even when asked to do an impromptu public speaking. Our troop went to a Wednesday evening vespers service, the only troop in the camp to do so, and the scout leader at the service welcomed us warmly. He asked for the youngest scout to come forward, and, with that being Liam, he popped right up there without hesitation. The leader explained that he always asked the youngest scout to say the opening prayer. "Dear Lord," Liam began, "We ask that you watch over all of us here at camp. We are having a great time, and ask you to keep us safe. Amen." I had never been prouder of him.

After return from that camp, Liam went to a golf camp for three days and then to a farm camp that he dearly loved. His headaches became a bit more frequent, but not intense and usually not requiring any medication. He mentioned that the back of his neck was a bit sore and that our nightly rubs helped the discomfort. Still, Michelle and I started to worry a bit. Michelle felt that he could use a visit to his pediatrician for a checkup, perhaps checking his blood sugar among other things. A vision check was also scheduled. Since he had absolutely no other symptoms (e.g., nausea or dizziness), and he continued his activities, we thought that these things would suffice.

The week before the Fourth of July found Liam in the second week of the farm camp. His headaches continued, and although we did not know it, his activity there was limited. He would tell us later that he had to go sit in the leader's cabin to rest on occasion. I will never forget a call we received from him out at the camp at lunch on Thursday, July 1. He called to tell us of another headache and asked about coming home. Now, my sister and her boys had arrived in town that day in anticipation of a Kentucky trip we were all taking the following day. I knew Liam wanted to visit with them and was hesitant about even going to the camp that day. I suspected he wanted out early to be with them and told him so. He denied it, saying that the reason was truly his headaches. I told him I would call him in thirty minutes and see how he was and if he were still not feeling well I would come get him. "But," I added with a hint of smugness, "You will come home and rest and not play with your cousins." When I called back, he had recovered as usual and was back at the camp.

The following day, my and my sister's family embarked on our trip, which would take us first to western Kentucky and then on to Memphis before returning to Nashville a few days later. Liam was feeling fine, riding with cousins in my sister's SUV, cutting up as usual. His appointments, with the pediatrician and the ophthalmologist, were all set for the week after our return. We were confident that the headaches would then be addressed and remedied.

Hello all,

As most of you have undoubtedly heard by now, our son Liam was diagnosed with a brain tumor on Saturday, July 3. He had been experiencing mild headaches off and on for 3-4 weeks but they had gotten worse the past few days. On the first morning in our hotel, I was awakened at 4:00 AM by a moaning sound. Thinking Liam was having a bad dream, I called over to him. "Liam, is that you?" He replied "yes" in the same agonizing tone. I asked him what was wrong and he said that his head was hurting. This was the first time he had any morning headache, which gave me a bit of heartburn. I got up, as did Michelle, and gave him a Tylenol. After thinking about options for a moment, I decided then to take him to a nearby ER in Paducah, KY. "I'm taking you to the ER," I announced, thinking we would put an end to these worries here and now. Perhaps we would find he did need glasses or that he was not getting enough fluids. "I'm going too" said Michelle. "I'm going back to bed!" announced my seven-year-old daughter Aubrey, never once to mince words but adding a bit of levity to the moment.

Leaving her in the charge of my sister, we made the short thirty-minute drive to the hospital. Little was said, as Liam's headache was improved. I learned later that Michelle was busy praying the rosary with her beads as she sat silently while I drove. We were checked in, labs were drawn, and a head CT ordered. The doctor there seemed a bit surprised at our presence, as it did not represent a true "emergency" in that sense, but he understood our concern. He returned about two hours later with the news that while all the labs were normal, there was "something" with the head CT that needed further study. "It may just be his anatomy," he explained, "but to be sure he needs a MRI. It may be a tumor, but we can't say that for sure." We had to go to the other hospital in town for the MRI, and after it was done we sat waiting for the radiologist. I have to admit I did study the MRI technician's facial expression after the study was completed, when she was taking the films to the radiologist for review. She must be an excellent poker player, because she gave absolutely no hint anything was amiss.

The radiologist summoned me back to his office a few minutes later, while Michelle had taken Liam to the restroom. He looked to me and said "I'm sorry. He's got a mass." I told him to wait, that I had to get Michelle so he could show both of us. When she returned, she could tell by my look that she needed to come with us. He showed us the golf-ball sized tumor, and she dissolved into tears. He went on about the types he thought it might be, and how sorry he was, that he had a son this age, etc. But the only information we needed was staring at us from his monitor screen.

We walked from the hospital, hand-in-hand with Liam between us, in silence. I immediately put on my "game-face," putting a call in to a neurosurgeon at Vanderbilt (near our home in Brentwood). His tone was matter-of-fact, stating he would put Liam on an oral steroid to reduce swelling and that hospitalization was not needed. Being a holiday weekend though, the soonest he or his partner could see us would be in four days. We made it back to the inn, exhausted mentally and physically. Liam took a nap, while Michelle and I discussed matters with my sister and uncle who were there. I then made a call to St. Jude Children's Research Hospital in Memphis. Having rotated there in 1987 as a third-year medical student, I knew of its reputation and stature. This knowledge was confirmed exponentially after their life-saving treatment of a close friend's daughter just four years prior (brain tumor). I asked the operator for the neurosurgeon on-call that day, using my title as the caller, and she put me through to Dr. Stefanie Einhaus. Dr. Einhaus listened to my story and told me to not delay. She said she would meet me the next day (Sunday, July 4, no less) at St. Jude's treatment area to review the films. She also mentioned that "it might be a JPA," which is a benign tumor that needed excision only, but that "it needs to be done this week," Since Memphis was on our travel agenda already, we kept it there and decided that we would see her the next day.

After that call, I walked outside the inn lobby where my uncle was standing. He had lost his wife of 38 years a couple of years prior to cancer, so he had an inkling of what we faced. For the first time, I lost all composure. When people provide hope and any sort of reassurance, as Dr. Einhaus and Uncle Don had done, I find that it hits deep inside me. All of my anxieties and worry about the diagnosis were released during those moments; no words needed to be said.

After composure, we decided to resume this vacation as close as originally planned as possible. This included a game of putt-putt golf that evening, as well as a day on the lake with friends the next day. Liam, though somewhat depressed at his diagnosis, was nonetheless free from the headaches and did the best he could with the activities.

We drove to Memphis, as planned, on the Fourth of July. Phoning Dr. Einhaus on the way, we inquired about when and where to meet. She asked if I had my family along, and I replied that not only my family but that my sister and her boys as well were coming. She said that her Sunday school class had a potluck area at a large fireworks show that was to take place that evening on the church grounds. We could meet there, she offered, get the kids something to eat and in place for the fireworks, and she and I and Michelle could steal away for a few minutes to review the MRI disk.

So here we were, at a festive 4th of July fireworks celebration and potluck amongst hundreds of people. A mom holding a daughter's hand with both of hers comes walking our way. Yep, that's our neurosurgeon, laptop in tow. We excuse ourselves and make our way into the church building so she can look at the MRI. "Hard to tell from this, but it may be benign. We'll have to see of course with the pathology at surgery." We return to our families and resume taking in the sights and sounds. Dr. Einhaus leaves shortly afterwards, having been summoned to the pediatric ER for emergent surgery for a tumor compressing a youngster's spinal cord. The fireworks conclude the gorgeous evening. Surreal.

Liam was admitted into Lebonheur Children's Hospital on the morning of July 7, and the operation got underway around 11:00 AM. Dr. Einhaus had told us to expect at least a six-hour surgery, given the delicate nature of removing the tumor (felt to represent a benign JPA). Telling Liam to "hang on" as they wheeled him down to the OR was the second hardest thing we've ever done. We went back to his room to wait out the afternoon.

We began receiving updates from the OR on the hour, but it was the third call from there that really got our attention. "The tumor is out," said the nurse. "Dr. Einhaus has begun to close and we should be finishing within the next hour." Wait a minute....wasn't this supposed to last at least another 2-3 hours? What about the preliminary path report? "Oh, Dr. Einhaus will be discussing that with you when she comes to see you there when she's done." Being a physician, I know what that means: bad news. I tried to prepare Michelle that the pathology was not what we had hoped, but the words from Dr. Einhaus still felt like a body blow. "It is a medulloblastoma, which unfortunately is malignant. He will need both radiation and chemotherapy." I could not take a deep breath. "I feel sure we got it all." Now what? Why? "If his spinal cord MRI is normal and there is no spread, his chance of surviving this is at least 85%." What do you mean, chance of survival? Was this really happening? "You can come see him in the ICU within the hour."

We went to see our little man in the unit, hooked to any number of monitors and IVs. He was still sedated, but he knew we were there. "I'm proud of you" I told him. He nodded. His mother kissed his forehead. "Okay" when asked how he was feeling. Then, it was time to leave.

There were no parent rooms available that night, and we were not allowed to sleep in the room with Liam. I knew that he would be in good hands that night and convinced Michelle to go with me back to the hotel for some semblance of sleep. Walking out of that ICU and hospital was the hardest thing we had ever done.

Back in our room that night, sleep was sporadic. The ICU nurse had told us that she would call us if the need arose, but that she did not expect any problems. Once, when were on the precipice of sleep, a phone rang. I shot upright in bed, only to be assured by Michelle. "It's the room beside us." Cheap thin walls.

Liam will now undergo an MRI of his entire spinal cord to check for spread, as well as a post-operative MRI of his brain to check for any residual tumor. We are prayerful that those studies will show no tumor spread or remnant.

So we will become a St. Jude family. The details of further treatment depend on final pathology reports and the above-mentioned studies. Liam is in the ICU tonight and will be transferred to a regular room tomorrow if he progresses as expected. We may be discharged as soon as Sunday-Monday (11th-12th).

We are most appreciative of your thoughts and prayers. That is what we need in the way of that question "what can I do". As specific needs arise, we are comforted by the fact that we can reach out to you.

Psalm 138:7

Chapter 2

St. Jude

Liam Hoover Update II

July 9, 2004

Liam has progressed very nicely and on schedule since the operation. He is now in a private room, and resting comfortably. He has done well with his neck exercises (needed due to expected post-op swelling and spasm), and even walked around the unit this evening with Shelley's and my assistance. He fatigues easily, but his pain level is improving daily. We hope to be discharged either Saturday or Sunday, with our subsequent return to Brentwood a day after.

Waiting in Liam's room the following day was almost at trying as the day of the surgery. Only this time, we were hanging on any news from the brain and spine MRI he had undergone that morning. He was in a suite, and I had stationed myself behind a partition, attempting to read. I did not progress more than a few pages, for each time the door opened I got up to see if it was Dr. Einhaus. I would then return to my post after seeing that it was a nurse/visitor/patient representative. As fate would have it, the results were delivered via telephone (a good sign, since she would have delivered bad news in person).

We were due for some good news, and received it in the form of the post-operative MRI on his brain showing no residual tumor. Additionally, his spinal MRI showed no evidence of metastasis (spread for the non-medical types). We discovered the real definition of exhilaration upon receiving this news. I could actually breathe normally for the first time in over 24 hours.

We are awaiting contact from St. Jude, who in turn is awaiting final pathology results of the tumor. We will also at least investigate the possibility of oncology treatment through Vanderbilt. We expect both radiation therapy and chemotherapy, as is the standard for these tumor types.

Liam is understandably a bit depressed, more physically we believe than mentally. Could not even interest him in looking at the "Calvin and Hobbes" book we got him. But he is progressing, and we know he will continue to do so throughout this entire ordeal.

It is difficult to put into words our experience this past week. For some reason, the term "gut wrenching" comes to mind the fastest. I'm sure you can think of several others. Nevertheless, the Biblical physician Luke wrote that we cannot change anything by worry, and we do try and keep that in mind. We continue to ask God for the strength to continue this fight and to accept His will.

Liam was discharged from the hospital on July 11, less than 100 hours after major brain surgery. We stayed in the hotel that night, and the next day we headed home to Brentwood (a city just south of Nashville). We were greeted there with a large basket of games and goodies, the first of many such gift items we would eventually receive. One of Liam's best friends came to visit, and although Liam was only able to converse from his perch on the couch, his friend was content to sit with him there. The chuckles he extracted from Liam were priceless.

Liam Hoover Update III
July 15, 2004

Liam has continued to improve. Coming home last Sunday (7/11) had much to do with that. His friends have come by and lifted his spirits, playing games and such. Of course, the plethora of goodies and games from our neighbors and friends helped bring a smile to him (and subsequently us) as well.

Other visitors included school representatives of his upcoming sixth grade class, who reassured us of their diligence to do whatever it took from their end to see to his success in school for the upcoming year. Also from his school, the high school football coach and an assistant took time out of their schedule and came for a visit, bringing along three of the seniors from the team. What's remarkable about these visits was the fact that although Liam had not formally matriculated to Brentwood Academy, he was already a part of their family.

St. Jude Children's Research Hospital was founded by the late entertainer Danny Thomas in 1962. Named after the patron saint of "desperate cases," it is one of the leading institutions in the world in the treatment of all types of childhood cancer. Every patient accepted at St. Jude is entered into a research "protocol," and cutting edge diagnostics and all-encompassing therapy are provided to every patient at no expense to the family. One's insurance (if insured) will be billed, but no charges are ever sent to a patient's family regardless of their financial situation. Moreover, St. Jude (through their fundraising arm ALSAC) pays mileage for those traveling by car and will pay for the patient and a parent to fly in for treatment if the distance is greater than 300 miles. There are three separate temporary residences set up for families (Grizzlies House, Ronald McDonald House, and the Target House) again at no charge. As one social worker put it, "No one wants to be here, but we make it as tolerable as we can."

I am writing this update from St. Jude, where we have decided to pursue further treatment of the cancer. One of the world leaders in researching and treating this type of tumor is located here, and the 225-mile drive is a relatively short hop for us (considering the variety of license plates in the parking lot). We met with this neuro-oncologist today, and knew just by his bedside manner alone we were in the right place. In addition, the support system here goes beyond words.

Four years ago, we were struck with the horrible news that a friend's daughter was diagnosed with a brain tumor. Her father and I had known each other since internship, served together in Germany and Desert Storm, and finally were residents together in San Antonio. Their daughter, two years

Liam's junior, had experienced headaches and dizzy spells for a few weeks. An MRI revealed the tumor, and surgery was done there in a local medical center. The pathology was that of a rare form of medulloblastoma, fairly recently assigned its own name (rhabdoid tumor). Only several hundred tumors of this type had been placed in this classification, and the type demanded fairly prompt oncologic evaluation and treatment. Told essentially that "there is nothing more that can be done" after an incomplete excision, the parents were despondent. We had discussed with them the possibility of contacting St. Jude's, and my friend called Dr. Amar Gajjar one day to ask for help. He may have used the words "Can you save my daughter?"

The answer was yes. Alexis and her parents flew to Memphis and met with Dr. Gajjar, a world leader in this particular type of pediatric brain cancer. He enrolled her in a research protocol that called for high-dose radiation to the brain and spinal cord, as well as a four-month intensive chemotherapy regimen. The agents used in the chemotherapy would so devastate the bone marrow's ability to regenerate blood cells that a modified bone marrow transfusion would have to be done after each cycle in order to boost said production. She completed the protocol in late 2000.

She just returned in January for her five-year checkup, free of any recurrence. Survivor, she is. Not some "reality" TV pretender.

Final details of the treatment plan are still pending, but in general the plan is as follows: Six weeks of radiation treatment (craniospinal – to both the brain and spinal cord), followed by a 4 week break. Then, 16 weeks of chemotherapy. The radiation sessions are outpatient, with weekend breaks so Liam can come home. The chemotherapy will be mostly inpatient, with fewer weekend opportunities. We will essentially relocate (two of us anyway) to Memphis from August to February, with the above-mentioned weekend returns home.

Liam has accepted his fate with trademark circumspection, and is a true example of courage for Michelle and me. Someone mentioned to us in an email that he is a child of God (as all children), and in that I find reassurance and a measure of comfort. Prayers offered for us from Alaska to Florida keep us strong as well.

One's first foray as a parent into the world of St. Jude is overwhelming, to put it mildly. We were still in sort of a daze as we saw infants and toddlers, pre-teens and adult-sized teenagers scattered throughout the facility. Careful not to stare, we could not help but notice the lack of hair, the transport wagons and crutches many of them need, the masks, and the IV lines disappearing into their shirts. I for one kept shaking my head in disbelief as we were led through the registration process, as if we would suddenly be given the news that a mistake had been made and that, upon further review, Liam's tumor was benign after all. We followed the printed daily schedule diligently, which included a thorough head-to-toe physical and imaging evaluation. From eye and dental exams, to cardiac echocardiograms and renal ultrasounds, to body-wide bone scans and neuropsychiatric testing—all systems were accounted for and extensively examined. Liam had a personal relationship with the MRI personnel, having undergone ten of those alone within his first two months from diagnosis. On the body fluid side of things, he had the usual blood and urine tests, as well as spinal fluid taps. All of these examinations revealed no evidence of any cancer spread, thankfully enough, but the protocol would not alter. He would undergo the same regimen as our friend Alexis.

He had the exact same tumor.

Chapter 3

"The Hulk"

Radiation therapy is an exact science. Liam had about a week's worth of preparation for the treatments, and had to sit still for his head to be fit into an outline (mold). In fact, his first treatment was delayed for a day for the radiation-oncologist to re-shape the mold (a multi-hour process). When I queried our neuro-oncologist about this, he mentioned that if a few centimeters of the brain were "missed" in the radiation process (such as around his temple region) then THAT would be the area where the tumor would recur.

Sobering.

Liam endured thirty separate radiation treatment sessions, which took only about forty minutes a day to complete. His entire brain and spinal cord were included with the initial treatments, with focused beam radiation on the tumor bed itself in the latter ones. This actually was perhaps the most important part of his post-surgical care, given the fact that his tumor type is extremely sensitive to the effects of radiation. Unfortunately, Liam's hair follicles and intestinal tissue were also sensitive, resulting in losses from each (hair and gastric contents). While a concern, we could not be concerned with long-term effects at this point. No, as one of his uncles asked, one of the effects would not be "Incredible Hulk" powers.

Liam Hoover Update IV
July 30, 2004

As we draw an end to the most trying month of our collective lives, we truly have much to be thankful for in terms of Liam's illness:

- *Liam's amazing recovery from the operation itself, with an intact neurological examination at every stage*
- *No evidence of spread of the tumor either in the spinal cord or in the spinal fluid*
- *Complete and total resection of the tumor under the capable hands of the pediatric neurosurgeons at Lebonheur Children's Hospital.*

That being said, we certainly have a daunting challenge ahead. Liam has completed two treatments of radiation to date, and has about 28 to go. It makes him a bit nauseous and fatigued, but that will pass. The treatments themselves only last about 20 minutes, and he gets one per day (Monday through Friday). The completion date will fall around the week of Labor Day, when he and Michelle will be able to come home for about a month. He will then join his 6th grade class until he has to return in October for the chemotherapy.

Liam continues to enjoy the cards, emails, and visits he receives. It means so much to him after being away from home going through what he has to. With your help we continue, to paraphrase the apostle Paul, "fighting the good fight".

Aubrey will remain in Brentwood, and we hope to keep her life as "normal" as possible. We know we will need to call on family and friends in this regard, and know we will receive the assistance we need. It goes without saying how awed we are at the generosity and support of the human spirit, shining through so many of you. We continue to appreciate your cards and emails, and as you can see will need the prayer network as we continue our odyssey.

Family separation is a challenge, especially for a daughter who needs her mother. Neighbors and extended family were gracious to assist in any way possible, and did, but I knew my daughter Aubrey missed her mother. Fortunately, she had the same second grade teacher as her brother, who was instrumental in her success in overcoming the challenges throughout the school year. Even at the age of seven years, her friends showed their spirit, as evidenced by this note given to her by one of her classmates:

Dear Aubrey,
I hope you are doing well. I'm glad that you are in my class.
I'm glad that we are good frinds(sic). If you want to play I will

call you or you can call me. You are always smiling you make me smile too! Tell Liam I said hi and that I'm looking out for you while he is gone. -Stephen M.

Liam Hoover Update V

In memory of Allison: "How long will we miss you? Only forever."
-Inscription on one of many donated wagons around St. Jude that are used, in place of wheelchairs, to transport those patients too weak or otherwise unable to walk.

In memory of Jonathan: Born to us 04/05/80. Born to heaven 11/11/91.
-One of hundreds of memorial plaques blanketing the St. Jude walls.

We are reminded daily of the challenge all patients and their families face. Liam has enjoyed more "good" days (defined as 1 vomiting episode or less) than bad. He has needed a couple of IV's for anti-nausea this past week; radiation has that effect on the gut when the spine is treated. He also becomes fatigued for a few hours after the treatments. We hope this improves in time.

Scared? Probably that is not a strong enough word. But knowledge is power. The world-wide web has made on-the-spot research only a few keystrokes away. We knew right away the outlook/prognosis for patients with Liam's tumor type, but we tried very hard to focus only on the positive. Still, the occasional discussion with another parent at St. Jude usually resulted in humility, such as the one with a mother and her son sitting across from us in the radiation therapy waiting room. Michelle and the mother exchanged pleasantries, and Michelle asked how her son was doing. His mother replied that he was doing well, having had surgery recently for a brain tumor. Michelle then said how Liam too had had recent surgery. The other mother then remarked that this was their second time through, having undergone an initial operation seven years ago when he was six years old. About three months ago, the tumor had recurred. He was now going through the radiation process *again*, following his second surgery. Another day, while Liam was an inpatient, Michelle was commenting on how Liam was a bit antsy to be discharged. He was coming up on day 5, his scheduled day for release. The other mother listened quietly, and answered "five weeks" when Michelle asked how long her son had been in the hospital.

I was reading a forwarded email update on one of my brothers' friend's son, who had been battling cancer now for about six years. The father had related that further chemotherapy was not an option because his son's marrow had been depleted after thirty-four cycles. Makes our four cycles look like a walk in the park.

Michelle and Liam have moved into temporary "digs" in downtown Memphis, a corporate apartment dwelling for the month of August. We decided to go this route for privacy reasons and for a need to get some sense of normalcy away from St. Jude when our day is done there. It is across the street from the Peabody Hotel, so perhaps they can watch the ducks parade down to the lobby on occasion.

Liam enjoys his time at home, as evidenced by his attendance at two birthday parties for friends of his last weekend (one a slumber party). He is holding up very well, all things considered. He is particularly excited about beginning 6th grade; his middle school has provided him with a laptop with a web-cam so as to tune in to his class periodically (and vice versa – the class can see what is happening with Liam).

Since I started this with a solemn note, I will end with an upbeat one: One of the neighborhood girls had a party, and in lieu of presents she asked for donations to St. Jude. The total take was $270. Stories like that warm hearts.

People want to help. That concept was reinforced time after time throughout our journey. Donations poured in from friends and families. Workers designated St. Jude as the recipient for company-donated funds from their paychecks. Birthday party receipts, an organized car wash, and participation in and collection of money for the St. Jude Marathon added to the generosity. While and exact total is not known, it is in the $15,000 to $20,000 dollar range.

Liam Hoover Update VI
Sep 1, 2004

Liam had another great weekend, highlighted by going on a hike with his Boy Scout troop. He plugged along for the entire 8 miles, half of it through a storm and the subsequent soaked trail. Moreover, he did this after having declined both breakfast _and_ lunch (due to his appetite wanes). Yet, after a good nap on the way home and a hot shower, he dusted off 3 waffles. He told me once on the trail that "Dad, I'm glad you're with me on this hike." Of course I could not answer because of that recurring lump in my throat.

We are now on the downhill slope of the radiation treatments, and Liam's last treatment will be September 10. Then, he and Michelle will be home for 4 weeks and we resume some form of normalcy. We will return to Memphis on/about October 11 to prepare for chemotherapy, which will initiate the following week.

The chemotherapy will be delivered IV (intravenously), through a semi-permanent "port" which will be placed in a vein under Liam's collarbone. The time frame is measured in 4 week (28 days) cycles. He will receive several agents throughout the course of the first 5-6 day period. On day 6, he will receive a transfusion of his own blood cells (known as stem cells) to stimulate the production of his red and white blood cells as well as platelets. Days 7 through roughly 25 (give or take a couple of days) will consist of Liam receiving daily infusions of a growth stimulating factor (also to boost production of the above-mentioned blood cells). The remainder of the 28 days will be the time when he may be able come home, provided his cell counts allow. This however may not happen due to his tenuous immune state; we do not want to tempt even a cold. He will undergo 4 of these 4-wk treatment cycles, putting a tentative completion date in early February.

No way around it, radiation is child's play when compared to chemotherapy. Not only are there immediate effects like nausea and hair loss (again!), but there are longer-term issues of endocrine damage and hearing loss to contend with. St. Jude is at the forefront however of limiting these effects, safely reducing dosages of some chemo agents as well as adding "protective" medications in with the initial 5 day chemo run. In addition, the team at St. Jude screens entire body systems routinely to monitor even the slightest need for intervention (for example growth or thyroid hormone).

WHY? It is easy to ask that question (and we have). But as I was reading from a book by the pastor David Jeremiah, a better question to ask is WHAT. As in, "What

Lord, would you have me do with this challenge?" Perhaps, Liam can serve as an
example for others by providing inspiration through his courage and reverence.
He can also use this experience for reflection whenever faced by future obstacles
life will present.
   As can we.

Neighbors of ours have a son who is on the Auburn University swim team, and his roommate was good enough in the backstroke to earn a spot on the 2004 Olympic team. Though he never met Liam, he was "introduced" to him and began an electronic mail correspondence. He also told our neighbors he would try and get Liam something from the team. A few days prior to the Games, a package arrived for Liam, with a T-shirt signed by all of the Olympic swimmers on the team, male and female. The note written to Liam told him to "pull for us in Athens, as we are all pulling for you."

Liam Hoover Update VII
October 2004

After spending 4½ glorious weeks at home, our family has again relocated to
Memphis as Liam returned to St. Jude on October 12. While home, he went to
school and seamlessly joined the rest of his class in their progression through the
6th grade. He even picked up some tennis strokes during his P.E., and did enough
homework and studying to pull off A's and B's at midterm. We hope he can stay
the course from afar as he was able to do throughout his radiation.

We were very concerned about the effects of radiation on Liam, having read about the cognitive defects and development delays that are all too common. The gastrointestinal and hair loss effects were obvious, but he did not show any ill effects with higher levels of brain function. This was evidenced by his amazing school work and the fact he could not only keep up with his class but that he excelled as he had never done before.

He thoroughly enjoyed playing with his friends, both from school and the neighborhood. One afternoon was spent helping the rest of his comrades from church washing cars (and each other), with the proceeds (over $2000) going to St. Jude. A neighbor engineered the entire process, right up to collecting donations from unsuspecting patrons at a party later that night. She is another shining example of THE light of the world we have witnessed throughout this journey.

Ah, and the news from 10/15 is good. We have received the "all clear" from reports on Liam's MRI's of his spine and brain, as well as his spinal tap that was done on this day. Psalm 100 certainly comes to mind.

Monday will bring the surgical procedures of the "central" line placement (detailed in the last update) as well as the bone marrow aspiration. The "stem cells" obtained from the marrow will then be cryogenically preserved and then "transplanted" into Liam after the 5-day run of the triple-agent chemotherapy. This will boost his immune system and allow for a quicker "recovery" in order to yes, do it again, three weeks later. The cycle repeats itself three more times (four total) before completion.

Liam continues to receive and enjoy the cards sent from near and far. While acknowledgment cannot be made on an individual basis, we hope that you know that we all appreciate the continuing prayers and words of support. Those contributions help Michelle and I on a daily basis as we reflect on each respective message. Liam too realizes he has quite a network out there, and (with our help) will one day somehow express his thanks.

Liam's sixth grade class accounted for the majority of the cards, letters, and other items he received. Each one of the sixty-plus students wrote him at least 2-3 times, with some sending gift items. One of his teachers put together a photo album of each classmate, with a touching handwritten message below each picture. A class of sixth graders from my mother's hometown in rural Alabama sent letters, each one written as if they had known Liam all of his life. One of the nurses who works with me (but never had met Liam) sent a card at least biweekly, each one with a personal note.

Liam Hoover Update VIII

Chemotherapy is a memorable experience, and not just for the side effects.

From day 1, a moment of levity: Liam received a number of supportive medications while in the hospital, mostly as a preventive against nausea. One of these was Ativan, a Valium-like drug that can make one drowsy and often a bit loopy. One afternoon I am reading, and the TV is tuned to a talk show or something and he is over in this nap/dream-like state like he had been most of that day. All of a sudden, he snaps awake and says to me "I'll bet you five dollars he misses it." I of course had this quizzical look, and he looks at me and then to the TV, and back at me. "Tell me you were watching a football game, and there was a field goal try and you said that you hoped he made it." I reply to him that no, I was just reading and not even watching anything. He sighs, leans his head back and says "I'm losing my mind" as he slips back to sleep. I stifle a laugh.

Later, a moment of gravity: He is in his bed and I am in an adjoining room for the night. The room is connected only via a window, but there is a monitor that is on similar to that which connects to the nursing station. I can hear what's going on in his room, but he cannot hear me unless I press down the call button. Around 2 AM or so, I hear him shuffling around in his room trying to use the bedside urinal (not an easy task when you are tethered to 2-3 IV lines coming straight out of your chest). So, I get up and walk down to his room to help him out. We finish his business, and I get him back into bed. I tell him to call me next time and he says he will. I get back in my room and have just lain down when I hear him call out "Dad". Thinking he needs me again, I start to get up. As I stand he finishes "...I love you". My day is made.

The first infusions of chemotherapy are now behind us, and now Liam is in the recovery phase. This portion of the cycle (3 weeks) involves waiting and watching. The wait is for his blood counts to rebound to acceptable and safe levels. The watch is for fever (which may indicate infection) and anemia (which may manifest as extreme fatigue and require blood transfusion). We expect him to experience either or both of these, as is the rule with the intensive chemo regimen he is receiving. Weight loss is another concern, and it is inevitable; but we try and limit it with appetite stimulants and the like.

We did not figure in the mental exhaustion of this process. Liam needs motivation to do most things (schoolwork, taking his meds; even getting out of bed some days). We have to balance our desire for him to do what he needs against the fact his blood counts are low, leaving him fatigued. At the end of the day, he is not the only one in that state. Yet, we only have to look to his seven-year old sister's insight for strength.

Michelle and she were reading one of the Berenstain Bears books a couple of weeks ago, and the storyline centered on the fact that there was a new baby in the house. Mama Bear was explaining to the older sister how the new baby needed a lot of attention, and that she did not mean to exclude or neglect her. After the conclusion, Aubrey said to Michelle "That's kind of like of us now. You and Daddy have to pay more attention to Liam because he is sick and away from home. And I'm OK with that."

We march on.

Sometimes, I could not help but think "does he *have* to go through with all of this?" I mean, he had no physical evidence of tumor/cancer since his surgery when the tumor was removed in its entirety. Was he going through living hell for prophylaxis? Then I thought that if he were to have a recurrence and we did not do radiation therapy or chemotherapy, I could not live with myself. Liam never questioned.

After the five-day hospitalization, Liam was released but not before receiving a bone marrow transfusion. Usually reserved for the blood-borne cancers such as leukemia, St. Jude employs this extraordinary procedure for faster blood count regeneration purposes. Without it, Liam's blood cell counts would rebound much more slowly. Now, he would recover in about three weeks, with the help of daily Growth Stimulating Factor (GSF), in time to get knocked down again with the next inpatient round of drugs. Yes, irony was a recurring theme throughout this entire process.

Our days out of the hospital were spent doing some schoolwork, daily hospital visits for clinic visits and the blood-cell-stimulating injections, and of course staying healthy. When his counts were below a certain level, an added level of protection was his wearing of a surgical mask. Despite the generous offer of free housing offered by St. Jude, in either the Ronald McDonald House or the Target House, we opted for privacy and seclusion and rented an apartment near the banks of the Mississippi River. We felt that the less exposure to young siblings running around the St. Jude housing, the better we all of us would be. Liam never had a sniffle.

Chapter 4

The Holidays

Liam Hoover Update IX

Psalm 118:29 is often quoted to reflect the feelings of the Pilgrims in the 17th century who engineered this wondrous holiday celebration. We too are thankful, despite the circumstance. Liam has continued to progress through treatment without major hiccups. We were delayed 4 days before beginning "Round 2" of inpatient chemotherapy due to a dip in his white blood cell count, thus necessitating Thanksgiving dinner from the St. Jude cafeteria. The meal was mediocre at best (think back to your elementary school mass-produced turkey), and we initially sat down to eat in Liam's room. After we started in, Liam rolled over in his bed and put his pillow over his head. Michelle asked him what was wrong and he said that he couldn't take that smell (of our food). So, we flipped the lids of our Styrofoam trays closed and shifted our meal to the parent room (a space about as wide as a walk-in closet). Thus, the basis for Aubrey's take of the holiday that "this was the worst Thanksgiving ever". I chuckled a bit, and reminded her of our blessings; then figured that out of the four Thanksgiving holidays that she can recall - this was the "worst" in her mind. Come to think of it, it ranks on down there for Michelle and me as well.

We did not wallow in self-pity for long, for Michelle happened to see a mother she had met from radiation. Her son, two years younger than Liam, was diagnosed about a week after Liam with the same tumor and location. Consequently, his treatment plan lagged Liam's by the same time frame. Michelle was a bit surprised that she hadn't come across them in clinic visits, and when she saw the mother this week she asked if they were in already for round 2. "We never left the hospital after the first round" was her reply, commenting that her son had endured complications from fever and thrush (a fungal infection of his mouth, throat, and esophagus). He needed intravenous nutrition due to not eating, and generally had not done well. It gives us a new perspective to our reply of "OK" when people ask how Liam is doing.

We have had a few celebrity visitors while in the hospital. David Green (a Busch-circuit stock car racer) stopped in during round 1, and Liam had his photo taken with Amy Grant not long ago. Brad Paisley and his wife Kimberly Williams came by this week, taking the time to tell Liam to come see him in concert when he got home. Liam will need to ask his daddy to go with him of course.

We look forward to December 4, when the St. Jude Marathon will take place. We have several friends coming down to run and support St. Jude in Liam's name, to include one relay team of his friends dividing up the 13½ mile half-marathon. We hope to stake out a spot between the hospital and our apartment to cheer them on (counting on decent weather and Liam's cell count status). We thank all in advance, both the runners and the contributors. We witness the result of your efforts daily.

Sitting in Liam's hospital room constructing this update, I have my headphones on listening to some MP3's when this Jars of Clay song begins. Yep...fitting.

"For those under the clouds, staring up in awesome wonder
As tears come slowly down, I'm reaching up a needful hand."
"Needful Hands"

St. Jude Marathon -

Liam Hoover is a vibrant 11 year-old sixth grader from Brentwood, TN. He has been forced to relocate though for most of the school year to Memphis. Liam was diagnosed with a malignant brain tumor in July of this year and is undergoing treatment at the world-renowned St. Jude Children's Hospital. This multi-building facility, founded in 1962 by the late entertainer Danny Thomas, has provided cutting-edge care to Liam and thousands of other cancer-stricken kids of all ages. Not only a treatment center, it is one of the top research centers in the world for all types of pediatric cancers.

St. Jude provides this care to patients at no cost (to the patient), and provides transportation costs to those who travel by air or by car. Housing is free, and a weekly grocery allowance is allowed for the families. The list of necessities provided by St. Jude is endless.

Of course, the dollars provided by St. Jude must come from somewhere, hence their fundraising arm ALSAC (American Lebanese Syrian Associated Charities; Danny Thomas was of Lebanese descent). One of the fundraising events is held each year in Memphis, and it is the St. Jude Marathon. Runners from around the world will congregate this year on December 4 to run in either the full or half marathon. Not only will these runners pay anywhere from $35 to $60 for this torture (I mean "experience"), they are looking to become "St. Jude Heroes". These individuals are looking to raise at least $250.00 in donations for St. Jude.

This is where you come in. This "hero" would like you to consider assisting in this endeavor toward the goal that has been set. Any financial help you can afford will be met with heartfelt appreciation, not only from this runner but also from the thousands of children (including Liam) who stand to benefit.

We met nearly all of the Brentwood half-marathon contingent and their family members at a famous Memphis Italian restaurant landmark. Liam was glad to see some of his buddies and had three of them over for a sleepover that night. Marathon day dawned sunny and clear, and we enjoyed watching all the runners come by at about mile 4, and then at the finish line a couple of hours later. We all met for some group pictures later, but Liam was by then just about to give out, so he napped back at the apartment while the rest of us met for lunch. Then we wistfully bade our friends goodbye, in that we wish we could also be returning "home" with them. For a few all-too-brief hours, we were a "normal" family again—laughing, communing, enjoying.

Liam Hoover Update X
Christmas Edition 2004

Psalm 16:3: And to the saints who are on the earth, "They are the excellent ones, in whom is all my delight."

You know who you are, you "excellent ones" in our life. You are the ones who have visited us in the hospital, who have visited with us at home. You have delivered thoughtful gifts and great meals. You have assisted in fund-raising for

St. Jude from birthday party proceeds to gift donations to helping wash cars. You came and ran, and supported those runners, in the St. Jude Marathon. (Note: Total donations to St. Jude from all the above are well above $10,000) You came to our house, put up and decorated our Christmas tree when we were in Memphis. Do I need to go on? I certainly can. You have helped take care of Aubrey at any time day or night. You have covered for me at the hospital whenever needed, and given me priority to set my own schedule there. You have written Liam countless heartfelt letters and cards, both traditionally and electronically. You have offered your prayers, lifting him (and us) upward, reflecting the true nature of God's people.

Liam has tolerated the 2ⁿᵈ cycle of chemotherapy better than the 1ˢᵗ, manifested by less nausea and a bit more energy. His appetite continues to be very good (though, curiously, for food more so than for his schoolwork). He was granted a 2-week "leave" from St. Jude, due his fast rebound and some holiday-related scheduling delays. Talk about the best Christmas present we could ask for... He will now be admitted around 12/29 for round three. We are officially halfway home (for good).

*2004 has marked milestones for us Hoovers. Michelle and I celebrated our 15ᵗʰ year in matrimony; we have come a long way from our Memphis/El Paso/Germany beginnings. My grandmother Hoover marked her 95ᵗʰ year, in as good as health as can be expected. Brad saw his 40ᵗʰ birthday come and go, with Michelle's to follow in 2005. Aubrey has responded remarkably well despite family upheavals; in a large part due to caring neighbors, family assistance, and a very supportive school structure. She is loving this adventure known as growing up, and although a little too fast for her mother and me at times. One thing, she is not one to mince words: At a Christmas concert not long ago, the singer sang "Have Yourself a Merry Little Christmas". Aubrey commented on how she liked the song, and then said "That's us. We're having a merry **LITTLE** Christmas" (referring to our 3-ft Christmas tree and the fact that we weren't decorating as usual). You can see we have our hands (blessedly) full.*

Oh, an afterthought. Our condominium in Florida was completely wiped out by Ivan the Terrible (as in hurricane), so we will have a brand new unit after insurance repairs. Perhaps in another year this would have garnered more attention and angst, but now we realize a bit more about priorities and what's important in this life. The sun will continue to shine.

Tears? Yes. Smiles? More. We await, with joy and expectation, the days of 2005. And beyond.

We were able to be home for Christmas, having encountered another admission delay the week prior. We found that our tree was up and decorated (no small task to do alone), and we set about finishing out Christmas cards and last-minute shopping. On Christmas Eve, we gathered around the Advent candles to ask for a special prayer. Aubrey chose to pray for Liam, as did Michelle and I, and Liam true-to-form chose to offer a prayer for Michelle's younger sister who was going through a bend in her road at the time.

We enjoyed Christmas and a couple of days after, then it was time to head west again. We were past second base, headed for third. No stopping us now.

Chapter 5

The Second Half

Liam Hoover Update XI

Intense love does not measure; it just gives.
Mother Teresa

"I have a son!" I remember clearly those words of sheer joy as Michelle phoned her friend minutes after she had given Liam his first bath. Talk about the apple of her eye...pick your metaphor...this kid has always had her heart. When he became ill, I was more than a bit concerned as to her reaction and state-of-mind. As it turned out, I had no reason for worry. Liam has met and exceeded the challenges that have surfaced in a large part due to his mother. She has become his daily nurse (dressing changes, line flushes), nutritionist (staying after him about his appetite and keeping his weight steady), and of course taxi driver (short and long distances). She dusted off her teaching skills for her greatest tutoring achievement in her career. Amazingly, he was able to stay with his class through the first semester from afar. He took all of his final semester exams on time, garnering all A's and one B in his courses. Her strength and resolve, grounded in her faith, have produced a wellspring of benefit for us all.

Three down, one to go. One knows they have been doing this too long when we get excited about the room layout, as Michelle was this time ("let's request this one next time!"). Liam and she rang in 2005 in the hospital (as did Dick Clark). Liam took in, at his mom's insistence, a New Year's Eve pajama party held for the inpatients. I believe he won a couple of Lego's in bingo.

He has become somewhat used to the hospital stays. Day 1 is always the toughest in terms of nausea, but he has this vomiting thing down to a science (apologies for the graphics):

- *Sit up and retrieve the bucket*
- *Let it fly*
- *Without looking up, hold up his hand for the waiting wet rag*
- *Wipe face*
- *Lay back in bed to resume previous activity (usually napping)*

Days 2-5 are not as taxing physically, but are quite monotonous mentally. He is a bit stir-crazy by the day of discharge, as are we.

Friday the 7th dawned cold and rainy, but that did not stop Liam's entire 6th grade class from paying a long-planned visit. We met them at a Memphis museum for a planetarium show, with Liam greeting his classmates as they got off two chartered buses (boys on one, girls on the other, plus all the teachers). We watched Liam's spirits being lifted at once, as you would've thought by watching those kids bounce off the bus that they were at the Magic Kingdom. After lunch there, we convoyed down to St. Jude where the kids visited the informative Danny Thomas Pavilion. The teachers were able to visit the hospital (only 16 and up can do so due to infection control reasons). We thought Liam looked a bit tired, but he held on during the entire visit. After they departed, he went for his clinic visit and needed a blood transfusion due to low counts. Superman.

I would like to borrow a closing that is put forth by another young cancer patient's family, who sends out daily updates on his progress. I was touched that the father, a friend of my brother's but whom I have not met, now includes Liam on his list. So, thank you for your prayers and for remembering Liam, Chris, Alexis, Blake, Ben, Sam, and all the young cancer survivors; along with those who have fought bravely against insurmountable odds.

Liam Hoover Update XII

Our patients have the cutest S.M.I.L.E
Our patents have the sweetest H.E.A.R.T.
O, we love to see you everyday
But now it's time we get to say
Pack your bags, get out the door
You don't need chemo anymore!

(sung, to the tune of the Oscar Meyer song, by the nurses for Liam in the hour before his discharge from his final round of chemotherapy)

Confetti, balloons, the song above, now THAT'S a party I am sorry I missed. The nursing staff and social work staff get together and throw a celebration for each patient who reaches the final day milestone. Liam added his hand-prints to the book of chemo finishers, kept by the hospital social work staff. He also received a shirt with "EOT" emblazoned on the front (stands for End Of Treatment). Michelle and I need a shirt like that as well.

Liam has spent as much time at home as he has in Memphis over the last two months. This is due to his remarkable health and stamina, and not needing the daily injections to boost his immune system. We were delayed a week getting into the hospital because of a shortage of available beds. Apparently, some kids had become ill with complications and needed admission. Irony: Being disappointed in having to go back home to Brentwood and resuming school and being with family and NOT being subjected to nausea, fatigue, muscle aches, sleep deprivation, etc. As my sister pointed out, however, we were thankful that Liam was not one of the ill patients needing the prioritized admissions.

Day #1 of the chemotherapy is always the hardest for him. He receives 4 separate agents and they all tend to make him sick, two of them in particular. This time, he probably heaved/vomited 10-12 times throughout the course of the day. Finally, about 5:00 PM that day he settled down and was able to rest, as was I. He coasted the next day, playing a war game on his laptop a friend had brought him and vomiting nary a time. On Fat Tuesday, the floor had their own Mardi Gras parade. Liam, at his mother's nudging, participated and enjoyed. St. Jude does not miss an opportunity to stage a party.

Liam and Michelle remain in Memphis, recovering from this round (as with prior rounds, receiving a blood transfusion or two as the need arises). He will have a final round of testing to include brain and spine MRI's, and yet another spinal tap, to ensure the continued absence of cancer. Following that, the next milestone will be getting his central IV line pulled out, an office procedure. We then pack up and hope to arrive home by the last week of February.
One "final" update to go....plus an announcement you won't want to miss... stay tuned.

Our excitement was palpable. The light at the end of the tunnel was growing brighter, day by day. And no train in sight.

In a medical school biology class, the random movement of cells was termed "Brownian Movement." Walk into St. Jude Children's Hospital and one will see the human embodiment of this process, with patients of all walks and physical appearances coming and going. The overhead paging system is constantly abuzz: "Alexis Huott to Assessment and Triage; William Hoover, please come to B clinic." "Ann Fitzgerald to the medicine room; the parents of Danielle Belousa to recovery please."

As we came to St. Jude on our "final" day, it was anticlimactic. Making our way to the clinic for the exit visit, we encountered new faces in the waiting room. We passed by one adolescent, probably thirteen, with a freshly shorn portion of his head visible. This assuredly indicated recent surgery and tumor removal and thus recent diagnosis. I recalled, on our first visit to St. Jude, seeing a completely bald patient like Liam was now, and thinking: I do not want my son to look like him," Now, counter-intuitively, I saw this new patient and thought the very same thing. He did not realize it yet, but he would trade places with Liam in an instant. Irony again raises its head.

All scans were clear, as well as the spinal tap, and Liam's central line was removed in a matter of seconds. He was glad to be able to pat his chest without fear of discomfort. We were rather unceremoniously released, with an admonishment to take it easy and "see you in three months." We snapped a couple of pictures with a couple of Liam's favorite nurses and made our way to the door. The hospital, for once, was rather quiet and devoid of the usual patient and family bustle. Yet the intercom continued, "...Alexandria Smith to C clinic please; Matthew Potter to the medicine room; Sharinda Gomez, please come to..."

Packing up and moving out of our apartment was quick and easy. We stopped and grabbed the last of the mail from the mailbox, and we were on our way home, for good.

A party was in order, to be given by us for all those who had walked and prayed with us along our walk.

Our Turn

It would be our honor to have you and yours join us in celebrating Liam's success in overcoming the greatest challenge of his 12 years. He, and we, would enjoy meeting and greeting the benevolent people in our lives that have prayed for us and thought about us in word and deed. The details:

Event: Hoover "thank-you" open house and celebration

Place: Holy Family Catholic Church, Gathering Area
9100 Crockett Rd
Brentwood, TN
Directions online at www.holyfamilycc.com

Date and Time: Saturday, May 7th; 1:30-4:30pm

Entertainment: All Night Long Productions Chuck Roberts, DJ
Bring your dancing shoes!

Refreshments provided (all of Liam's favorite junk foods!)

What to Bring: Yourselves

We are planning a short video montage depicting our journey, with comments by Michelle, Brad, Aubrey, and of course, Liam.

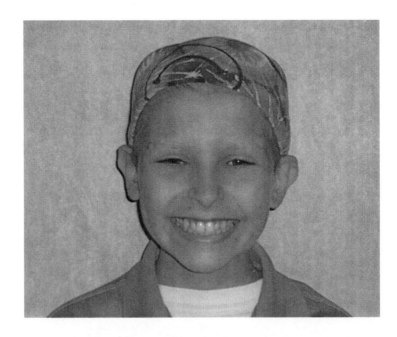

It was a wonderful celebration of life, attended by many with smiles all around. The popcorn and cotton candy machines were a hit with the young crowd, and the "limbo" brought out some body contortions several of us have not tried in years. We saw friends from near and far, and acquaintances old and new, all bound together by the common thread of thanksgiving and optimism.

End of Story

May 2005

I debated a bit on the title of this last update, as I cannot say our journey has "ended". Oncologists do not speak in such finalities when discussing the end of treatment with this tumor type. Instead, a time frame of no recurrence is a "disease-free interval"; no mention is made of the word "cured". Liam will be periodically assessed via MRI's and spinal taps until he reaches the age of 21. The schedule is, like the treatment he has endured, aggressive: Assessments every 3 months for 2 years, then every six months for 3 years, then annually. He will join the many vivacious-appearing teens and young adults we have seen coming in for these follow-ups, all with full heads of hair and looking quite "cured" to me.

Cancer of course has altered our lives, not only for the last 35 weeks but also for the foreseeable future. We will find ourselves uneasy with every headache or fever he will ever get. Our breathing patterns will shorten ever so slightly after each MRI and spinal tap he undergoes, until they resolve when we hear of the normal results (as we did this week). We will commiserate in spirit with parents of children newly diagnosed, and appreciate their absolute fear and trepidation of what may lie ahead. We understand Job 1:21 a bit more.

Lance Armstrong speaks of the "obligation of the cured" in his book It's Not About The Bike. As you know by reading these updates, we have been the recipients of so many offerings of good will and gestures of faith. Donations to St. Jude in Liam's name are nearing the $15,000 dollar mark if not more. In turn, we feel we are responsible for assisting others faced with this diagnosis or other types of problems that are sure to be encountered by any one of us in the future. No one is immune. As we were leaving St. Jude (March 4ᵗʰ), after Liam's central IV line was removed and all end-of-treatments scans and tests were normal, we stopped by the "medicine room" to say goodbye to a couple of nurses Liam got to know well. They were glad to see us, and we took a couple of pictures to mark the occasion. Another mother, from Williamsburg VA, noticed, and remarked how happy she was for us. She went on to say that her child was being treated for the same tumor type as Liam. I know she must have been inspired by Liam's celebration and success.

We hope to share our story with as wide of an audience that will listen. After some thought and listening to some of you, I have decided to put together a manuscript of our "bend in the road" and see where (or if) it goes. I do feel it may be of some help and consolation to another family or individual that may experience a similar situation. Anyone with publisher connections or suggestions, step forward!

We are again one family, under one roof. Liam is back in school, and back in play. Aubrey is glad to have her mother home. We are thrilled to be together, playing "Clue" on a Friday night. In closing, I reflect back to a Sunday of my youth. During our Communion service, the minister would recite a Bible verse as a section of the congregation would recess back to their respective pews. That day he recited Matthew 11:28, Jesus' invitation to "Come unto me all ye that labor and are heavy laden, and I will give you rest". Apropos, wouldn't you say?

We rest.

Chapter 6

Another Bend

June 2005

Hello to all. Since my "final" update of three months ago, Liam has successfully completed 6th grade, garnering 4 A's and 2 B's in the process. He has enjoyed being home and resuming his friendships, to include venturing into the paintball and air-soft realms of play. We all thoroughly enjoyed meeting and greeting some of you on May 7th, at our "celebration" event held at our church. For those who could not be there, I am still in the process of, well, processing a video montage of the event to share.

About 5-6 weeks ago, we noticed two small "lumps" under his skin on the back of his neck. About the size of a dime and quarter, we thought he may have developed a couple of cysts due to the weight of his backpack at school. I was in contact with his physicians in Memphis, who initially felt they were not serious but to keep an eye on them. We did, and they stayed about the same for the next 4 weeks or so, and did not cause him any discomfort. Over the past week or two, they grew in size and coalesced into one golf-ball and a half size mass. We felt (hoped) it was inflammation and/or a skin abscess, and knew the team at St. Jude would address at our 3-month checkup this week (6-9 June).

They (the neurosurgeon who did his initial surgery and his neuro-oncologist at St. Jude) were immediately concerned at the size and appearance, and scheduled surgery at Lebonheur for the 10th. Michelle and I began to feel the all-too-familiar sense of dread, but did our best to think positively. After all, for the tumor to recur in the skin was so rare that even Dr. Gajjar had not ever seen it (and he's been a specialist in this tumor type all of his adult life). Nevertheless, the possibility was real and our fear, palpable.

And realized. The tumor removed is felt to be the same type that was removed from his brain 11 months earlier, and about the same size. Talk about another sucker punch that we never saw coming. As for a silver lining, there is one. This tumor was confined to the soft tissue of the neck; his brain and spinal cord are clear. The neurosurgeon felt she got all of this one out in its entirety, and the tumor margins (areas around the tumor site that were biopsied as well) were clear.

As before, we do not know what the future holds. The strange this is, the doctors do not either (yet). They will meet and conference next week, after the final pathology results. They will research what very little is known about this type of "local" recurrence, pending the final path report, and communicate their recommendations. I suspect, at the very least, chemotherapy will be employed as this was alluded to by Dr. Gajjar. The thought of tackling that again is more than we can bear at this point. As for now, we are again focused on Liam's recovery, and are gearing up for that challenge.

Psychologically, this one's tough. We were just putting our lives together again, and only wanting to enjoy the summer we missed in '04. Liam has been through so much, as you all are aware. Yet again, we are appreciative to our prayer and support network as we negotiate this latest turn.

Tough indeed. We had encountered patients at St. Jude who were there, unfortunately, for "round two" of their disease. One youngster, thirteen years old, had his first tumor at age seven and now was going through the process again (surgery, radiation, chemotherapy) after a recurrence had been noted on a MRI scan. But three months later? We hardly had time to catch our collective breaths, and here we were facing cancer again. The fact that this was so rare that the brightest minds at St. Jude (and, the world) were unsure about why and even what it was only magnified our concern. "God, just leave him alone. Leave him alone!" I pleaded after realizing the potential cancer return. "All he wants to do is LIVE!"

There is little I can think of that is worse for a eleven-year-old boy to do on the first weekend of summer than to be sentenced to a hospital room, doing little more than nap and watch TV. At least Michelle and I could rotate shifts, reading and watching the clock on the wall, but Liam never offered one word of complaint or despair. Except once, matter-of-factly, when he remarked "I am missing [boy scout] camp this week, aren't I?"

I was incredulous at the notion that the lumps on the back of his neck could even be considered cancerous. After all, there was *no* mention of this type of tumor ever recurring beneath the skin in the literature; it had never been reported before. Right up until the time the surgeon came into our room with the news that it was indeed a tumor, I was confident it would be an infected abscess or scar tissue. I still shake my head.

Agony

Agony n. - intense pain of mind of body; anguish; torture.

Webster, of course, got it right.

We have been on an emotional string for the last two weeks since Liam's operation to remove the mass from the back of his neck. After a three-day stay at Lebonheur Hospital in Memphis, recovery from this surgery was quicker than the first one. He did require a small skin graft, taken from his upper thigh, to cover part of the incision along his neck. That has limited his swimming and other roughhousing activity, but the graft and incision are healing as expected. He went to his beloved farm camp last week, where he and his friends helped with the animal chores and played a bit in the creek.

Meanwhile, we were studying the caller ID for "ST JUDE" each time the phone rang, hoping to hear of confirmation concerning the final pathology report. On a follow-up visit Friday (6/24), we were initially told that the tumor type appeared to be that of the brain tumor removed 11 months prior. Additional cycles of chemotherapy would be in order. That news, including the requisite need for another central intravenous line and all of its restrictions, was enough to dissolve Liam into tears. Knowing what he endured before made this news so acute for him. "I just want my normal life back" was his plea, and ours.

After that, he underwent his routine spinal tap (clear), and later he had CT scans of his neck/chest/abdomen and pelvis to check for any spread of the tumor. While preparing for the scans, his physician informed us that new stains on the pathology indicated a change in the diagnosis. Instead of the original brain tumor type, the pathology indicated a sarcoma (a new primary tumor). This placed even more emphasis, and intestinal churning, on the CT reports. Normal! Talk about a roller coaster of emotions.

What exactly does this news mean? Our question, too. I'm not certain as to whether the diagnosis is good news or bad. Probably neither. Subtype analysis, differentiation of the precise type of sarcoma, will be ready sometime next week. Subsequently, a treatment plan will be spelled out. We are relieved of the fact of no visible mets (spread), but also realize that chemotherapy remains very much in the cards. The impact on the remainder of his summer activities, to include a much-anticipated two-week trip to the Boy Scout National Jamboree in late July, is unknown. We have reverted back to the "one day at a time" regimen.

The late psychiatrist Dr. Kubler-Ross described the stages of acceptance of life-altering news, and we have lived each of them in this journey. And here we go again: Denial (...this is really just an infected abscess or something like that), Anger (...how could this happen so soon after completion of therapy?!); Bargaining (...we'll come back every month for re-scans if we can avoid chemotherapy); Remorse (see above); Acceptance (still working on it).

We will find solace and strength again, through His hand offered by you. A prayer chain of neighbors is in full effect, generated by one who has suffered tremendous loss herself just two months ago. I know the nationwide call to arms is being sounded again.

Matthew 27:46 has relevance. But we hold to Psalm 31:3.

The battle is joined.

Yes, we certainly felt forsaken, but we knew of course that we were not. The very thought of having to endure chemotherapy together, with the requisite separation of my family when Liam had to be at St. Jude, was just about more that we could stomach. The impact had already been felt, with Liam and me having to miss the Boy Scout camp that we had attended together one year ago due to his operation. Instead, we were sentenced to a hospital room for the weekend, waiting for the hour hand on the wall clock to rotate enough times to the point when we could be released.

The spinal tap results weren't devoid of a bit of unneeded drama. The pathologist initially saw two malignant cells on the slide, but Dr. Gajjar felt that they were most likely of no importance given that patients who had undergone radiation were prone to have a few cells floating around. So the tap was repeated. I thought I would go bananas waiting on those, and the CT (neck, chest, abdomen) reports. When the NP relayed the clean readings, only then could I resume my normal breathing pattern. Time to head home.

Road Map

Returning home yet again along a lonely stretch of Interstate 40, we have concluded a trying week of testing and consultations. Earlier in the week, we shared in the good news of our Texas friends, whose daughter received the "all clear" from her visit (now five-plus years clean). We ran into our friends from San Francisco in the latter part of the week, there for Ben's 3-month check. We became acquainted with his family during our initial journey. His tests were normal, and Liam high-fived him on his way to the airport shuttle this morning as we headed toward the hospital for day surgery. Bittersweet had ne'er a better description.

Liam has his line (again) in place, but this time it will allow for a bit more freedom. It is a subcutaneous port, meaning it lies completely beneath the skin of his left upper chest. This will allow him to shower and to even swim, and does not carry the burden of daily flushes and cleanings. Other preliminary studies were completed, to include a bone scan, a bone marrow biopsy, and something called a PET scan (all to check for tumor spread). He had to have a repeat spinal tap, due to the one last week having two cells in the sample that appeared malignant. However, his neuro-oncologist felt that they were contaminants, floating around and left over from past radiation treatments, and repeated the tap. The repeat spinal tap was normal, as was the bone scan. The results for the bone marrow biopsy and PET scan should be available next week. Naturally, with every test we experience a new realm of unease, awaiting results.

On to the plan: Liam will undergo chemotherapy yet again, only this time for a much longer duration if his bone marrow allows (it still hasn't fully recovered from what he received this past year). His new physician overseeing his care, a sarcoma specialist, has carved out a therapy plan specific for Liam given his recently completed treatment. Standard sarcoma therapy is for 42 weeks (yes, 10 months), and his treatment schedule calls for chemotherapy sessions every three-four weeks over that time frame. The "standard" time frame though is in of itself arbitrary, and Liam's blood counts will be closely monitored before he begins each cycle. If his counts do not rebound consistently within the three week interval, then therapy will likely be aborted. Six months of therapy is felt to represent a decent goal for him. Radiation will be initiated around the end of August, again for 5-6 weeks and directed solely at the neck area where the latest tumor was removed. The radiation will be done at St. Jude, given their experience with Liam last year and for continuity of this vital area of therapy.

Fortunately, he will be able to receive the majority of the chemotherapy at Vanderbilt. While not formally associated with St. Jude, the pediatric oncologist there trained at SJ and knows the physicians there well. They have communicated and will coordinate Liam's treatment schedule so that the same agents and dosages will be given. This will be so much better on us as a family, and for Liam to be able to put his head on his own pillow at night.

Life goes on. We have arranged for the chemo schedule to allow him and me to attend the National Scout Jamboree later this month. He should be near the top of his game and recovered from the initial cycle, which starts next week at SJ. 7th grade will again prove to be a challenge, but the support demonstrated all too well last year by his school has not wavered. He will be in class whenever he is able. Liam does seem to have this all in perspective, better I will admit than I do. On the way back, I was temporarily tailgated and hounded by an aggressive driver. I responded in kind, and later apologized to Liam for my behavior and response. I told him that I would not have done that had this been a "regular" day. "Dad", he responded, dismissing that excuse, "Right now, there are no regular days."

I think we'll change his name to Solomon.

As you might expect, Michelle and I have wrestled with anger directed at God for not answering our prayers and pleas for Liam not have to endure this journey again. So many of you have sensed our despair and sent encouraging cards and emails, interceding on our behalf, and for that we are most appreciative. This most recent trip to SJ has brought us a sense of peace in that we have the diagnosis and the course of treatment. Again, we are surrounded by phenomenal physicians directing Liam's care, friends and family enduring this journey along with us and a God that understands, comforts, and gives us the power to persevere.

"Take courage, fear not. Behold, your God...will save you." Isaiah 35:4

It is impossible to characterize the utter stress of awaiting MRI and CT scan results of the most precious being in your lives (at that very moment). I try (then, try **not** to) read the faces of the technicians performing the studies for any clue as to what he or she might have picked up. Thankfully, they kept their best poker faces when we saw them – not that they were trying to conceal anything from us anyway. But awaiting the results is absolute torture, and then a normal result is verbalized to you as if commenting on the weather. Or, worse, it is not in hand: "Oh, I had it somewhere. Let me look for it and call you back." Normal results are often communicated in that nonchalant fashion; I am guilty of the same thing in my practice. It's part of that "detached concern" that is espoused during our training I guess. As a patient though, it detaches one from your body until you hear something.

Underway

You told me to call
Said you'd be there
And though I haven't seen you
Are you still there?

"Never Alone" by BarlowGirl

Heard that song, via earphones, while driving (alone) to Memphis to see what lay in store for my child. How do teenage girls write such stirring music?

Liam has begun the long road of chemotherapy, and none too soon. Though counterintuitive, we were never more ready to get the toxins started. A month ago, he had a lymph node pop up on his neck. Normally, this would be expected in one with a concomitant upper respiratory infection as he had; but, as we all too well understand – all bets are off when you are dealing with malignancy. The node was removed and was in fact cancerous, same type as the neck mass removed a month prior.

Though disconcerting, it really has little impact on his therapy plan, other than now this particular area of his neck will also be radiated during that phase of treatment. We have arranged to have his 2nd cycle of chemo to be administered at Vanderbilt, the day after our return from Virginia (Jamboree). Radiation will be sometime around the end of August and last through mid-October, and it will coincide round #3 of chemotherapy. That leg of the journey will be at St. Jude, and then most if not all subsequent chemo will be given again at Vanderbilt.

Liam has tolerated the first cycle of chemotherapy reasonably well, with few side effects. The medications given were selected in anticipation of his upcoming travel, hoping to avoid the anemia and fevers sure to follow with subsequent rounds. We enjoyed our Jamboree trip, despite the tragedy of the electrocution accident and the heat problems. Liam realizes his limitations, and did not overexert himself or experience any difficulties (other than being away from his mother for 2 weeks, though I'm not sure who missed whom the most). He learned to scuba dive (the first in our family to do that), and also enjoyed the Army Adventure Area and all of the military toys and vehicles. I think his favorite activity though was trading patches with youngsters from all over the nation; he now has quite a collection. He also met a couple of new friends.

In other news, our nearly-reconstructed condominium in Navarre Beach was the recipient of the menace from (Hurricane) Dennis. It was flooded out (again), but as long as the building is standing it can't be worse than the total loss from his brother Ivan just 10 months ago. Thankfully, we had not had the opportunity to move our furnishings in, thus sparing that expense. The fixed-income folks there who are trying to live a life of retirement are the real sufferers. I'm not sure how much more they can take.

Turning in the night prior to the hurricane landfall, I paused in amazement at our recent misfortunes. The recurring question "Why?" popped into my head. I am making my way through the Good Book (at my own pace – took me six years the first time, as a teen), and that night I happened to close out the book of Esther in the O.T. I flipped over to see what book was next before I clicked off the light. Whoa, I thought, there's my answer... (Job).

I do like the way that one ends.

Liam and I had a father-and-son experience in northern Virginia like none other we had ever experienced together. From the moment I saw that little fellow walking with his troop toward RFK Stadium for a Nationals baseball game until he climbed aboard the bus heading home two weeks and two days later, I was ecstatic. I made it a point to see him every day while at the Jamboree, despite my staff responsibilities and requirements. We did not do a whole lot of "interesting" stuff (except trade patches); he would get a bit tired by 1 or 2 o'clock and would need a nap. I was content to watch him do so. We would ride around the compound, and he would fiddle with the XM radio and listen to "Double Dutch Bus" or something similar. I don't know that I saw him more excited the entire time than when he was in the water during the SCUBA lesson.

The guys in his troop were great; one told me "I will see to it Liam gets around while here; even if I have to carry him on my back." Liam helped with the chores around his camp just as everyone else; I think he detested "K.P." the most. I was determined during those two short weeks to spend as much time with him as possible, and though I was well aware of the vagaries of cancer, I was not consciously sensing any impending doom. Not yet.

Chapter 7

Crash

Up and Down

What a difference a week makes with chemotherapy. The morning after his return from the Scout Jamboree (Aug. 4), Liam went into the hospital for a 24-hour stay for chemotherapy (3 agents). He got out about 5 pm, and immediately requested to join some of his school buddies at a sleepover. He had no restrictions, so off we went to the farm where the boys were congregating. They stayed up chatting that night and got up the next morning and had played paintball. Liam was on top of his game.

And then, the downturn. As expected, his blood cell counts dropped on schedule 7-8 days later, and with it came the symptoms of overwhelming fatigue and appetite loss. He could hardly raise his head from the pillow from his spot on the couch. He then developed a fever, necessitating an admission to Vanderbilt for antibiotics (13th-17th). Fortunately, he had no bacterial disease process, and began to feel better almost immediately. He also received blood and platelet transfusions, nothing new for him. Surely (we pray), if his marrow cells are wiped out, then any cancer cells present will bite the bullet along with them.

Liam has begun 7th grade, and will attend when he feels able. He and I have returned from St. Jude (chemotherapy cycle #3), and his bare head is now marked with "X's" for the upcoming radiation. Those treatments will begin around mid-September, and will continue until the end of October. The radiation will only be targeted at the areas of the neck where the 2nd tumor and the lymph node were removed. Either Michelle or I (mostly, she) will remain in Memphis on a Mon-Fri schedule during the radiation, returning home on weekends.

Watching your child endure such trials is unspeakably difficult. It is easy to slip into despair, fighting for every ounce of weight gain (or loss prevention). We rue the fact that he is not able to participate in everyday life events (school picnics, parties) due to his condition. Negative thoughts are always creeping around, fighting to get in our minds.

Yet, as before, we march on. Family and friends are in lock-step with us, in spirit and in person. The prayer pager is constantly a-buzz, and we are uplifted daily by notes, emails, and words of support and care. His cousins in Texas man a lemonade stand, with proceeds to St. Jude. A special nod goes out to my partners at work, "in the pit" of the emergency department, who are always willing to sacrifice their plans for my family needs at the last minute. And take time out from a busy shift to offer a prayer.

Liam will unknowingly provide comfort whenever he is able. He and I were playing word association the other day, waiting for another St. Jude appointment. "Aubrey" I would say; "Blond" was his answer. (I was expecting worse). "Pretty": "Mom" (still no. 1 in his book). "Life" I said. His reply: "Stinks". He then chuckled and said, "Oh, I'm joking. It's not so bad."

"How so?" I inquired.

"Well, I got family to cheer me up and all."

For the first time during any of his treatments, I was teetering on despondency. Liam had seemed to be recovering more slowly this go-around than the first rounds a few months ago. It was understandably explained that his body was already worn down from those initial cycles and that we should expect him not to bounce back as easily. While at St. Jude, I was about half-expecting the radiologist-oncologist to walk in and tell me that we could not schedule the radiation because they had found something new on the CT scan they had taken. Those negative thoughts had not found their way to the forefront of my mind in the past thirteen months, but Liam had never felt as weak during the initial chemotherapy as he had been in the past three-plus weeks. None of his physicians shared my fears, however, explaining that even if he hadn't had chemo before, that this protocol would take such a toll on anyone. Unfounded, I tried to reassure myself, as I tried to rid myself of this pessimism.

We left the hospital in the early morning after his chemotherapy ended around 5 am or so, and I was scheduled to work later that day. I was physically and emotionally spent, and asked my partner if he could cover for me the rest of the day. He said of course, and then offered me something much more substantial – a hug. For only the second time since all of this had begun a year prior, I broke down then and there.

Setback

As most of you know by now, we made an emergent trip to Vanderbilt after Liam had seizures on the morning of 8/31. The initial scans (CT and MRI) have indicated return of a tumor in a portion of his brain (above his right ear). After a couple of days of recovery, Liam was released after his confusion cleared up and his seizures were controlled by medication. Discussion and in-depth consultation between the physicians at Vanderbilt and his doctors at St. Jude are in progress, and recommendations and options are to be presented to us next week.

I have long feared this day. Having seen such progression and presentation in my practice, I could not help but wander to the "what if..." phrase as it pertained to my son. I was more worried about the latest neck tumor (sarcoma), given that his brain MRI was clear back in June. Realizing all unpredictability when it comes to malignancy, I made it a priority for him and me to attend the Scout Jamboree together. We enjoyed precious moments of father-son time during those two weeks, and I cherished every last one of them.

Anguish does not begin to describe our feeling. The fear is palpable. Michelle has redoubled her resolve, and is relying even more on her faith to see this through. Yet, the saddest picture I have ever seen is her curled up on Liam's bed the evening of that very long day, blinking back tear after tear. Hope is not lost, but confidence in Liam's healing has been shaken.

I'm not superstitious, but have become to believe in spiritual messaging. Just in the last two weeks:

- *I stumble upon a podcast of "A Word from the Word", a daily two-minute message from Rev. Dan Hayden out of Orlando. He happens to be delivering his messages this month from 1 Corinthians 15, with its emphasis on death and the resurrection. I had that on in the car a couple of weeks ago, and*

Dr. Hayden's message was "Falling Asleep". I have attached the file here: http://awordfromtheword.org/audio_files/WW8919.mp3

Liam was in the car with me but I was not sure that he was even listening, did hear it and commented "Oh, that's cool."

• At the Life Teen mass last Sunday, which we usually do not attend, a particular song (Be Not Afraid) spoke directly to us. "...blessed are you that weep and mourn for one day you shall laugh..."

• An article on faith and prayer in the April '05 Reader's Digest I was reading that day while in the MRI room with Liam: "Psychologically, prayer can organize anxieties, focus worries, offer a sense of comfort and connection, and solidify communities. But in the end, prayer is ultimately about realms of consciousness as yet unexplored--about what believers might call the soul, or the spirit, or some transcendent part of being. Some believe that prayers are actually answered. But it doesn't really matter: For those who believe, that is not where the true power of prayer will ever reside."

Our hope today is for Liam to be comforted, and not be afraid. He perceives when we are upset, so we fight to maintain our composure in his and his sister's presence. We will bring them along with these latest developments on their own time, as we strive to keep a sense of normalcy in our home. We rely on your prayerful support more than ever.

"BRADLEY!" A bloodcurdling scream from Michelle brought me bounding up the stairs to Liam's room, where she had been assisting him in the bathroom. I turned the corner into his room to see the nightmare I hoped I would never see: my helpless son involuntarily twitching and his helpless mother standing over him in horror. 911. Lights and sirens: I had no idea how to act on the other side of that action.

Good grief. Wait, strike that. There is nothing good about it. On the evening of Liam's seizures, I went home to swap places with Michelle as she would spend the night in the hospital with him. Prior to that, I had spoken with Liam's oncologist, who delivered the news that I wasn't all that surprised to hear: the cancer had spread to involve his entire brain membrane covering (leptomeningeal metastasis). My question to him was simple: Had he ever had a patient, of known of one, to survive this type of recurrence? He slowly but gently shook his head. How much time was pure conjecture. My brother was there with me, and I leaned on him for support, and guidance: How would I tell his mother? I drove home in silence, contemplating that question. Michelle and I had a few minutes alone in the house, and after I told her what the oncologist had told me, we simply broke down together. Trying to comprehend the terminal phase of his illness, we cried out loud as we realized what lay ahead. "Liam does not deserve anymore of this God-forsaken world" I shouted. "I can't live without him" sobbed his mother. We decided right then and there that there would be no casket or viewing but that Liam would have a beautiful memorial service instead. Michelle mentioned how she desired perhaps to have his cremated remains scattered out in the Gulf of Mexico since he loved being at the beach. We decided we would not divulge the fact that recovery was now impossible with either him or Aubrey. We sat, incredulous and dumbfounded, at one day's turn of events.

How does one prepare himself for the death of your child? Michelle set her mind and heart on a miracle, but I was not inclined to think much in those terms. Given my medical knowledge, I knew all too well the implications of this downturn. The immediate concern was whether or not Liam would recover enough to make it out of the hospital. He was mostly out of it for the first day, but he did wake up enough on day #2 to be placed on a regular floor. He did have his moments of confusion, at one time motioning for his sister Aubrey to come into the room; it happened to be his nurse just outside the door charting. The next day, I asked him why he did not want to watch TV at that time, and he replied, "My piano teacher Miss Paula does not want me to." She was his piano teacher...two years prior. He was released the following day; then the real challenge began. Would he seize again? Would his sister witness anything that she couldn't handle? Would we?

I put an immediate call into my mother in Birmingham and sister in San Antonio, imploring them to come ASAP. It went unsaid, but understood, that it would be a final farewell. They came over Labor Day weekend, and we strived for as much normalcy as possible, even having a family and friends cookout on the holiday itself. Liam hung in there with us, on round-the-clock steroids and anti-seizure medications. His younger cousin asked him once for assistance with putting together a Lego© toy. Liam did so, eliciting an admiring response "Liam, you're the greatest!" as he ambled off.

We had two weeks at home together before the end. Liam endured near constant vertigo and fatigue, to the point that last weekend where even watching the TV was not possible. I placed an urgent call that Saturday to his oncologist at St. Jude, imploring him to initiate any palliative treatment possible. He agreed to set something up the following week as long as Liam's blood counts had rebounded. My son was fading fast.

Thankfully, Liam did not experience any pain (headaches, etc.) and never once questioned if he would ever get better. We decided that we would not disclose any more information than either he or Aubrey could comprehend, and the subject of mortality never surfaced. I would just keep telling Liam "we have got to get you feeling better" and he would just nod. And understand.

The final day at home I had taken him to the clinic for an evaluation for dehydration as he had eaten and drank very little over the weekend. He was given a bag of intravenous fluid, did feel a bit better, and even ate some chicken nuggets on the way home. Later however, he could not hold those down or even a few bites of his last supper (chicken and rice). The next day would be his last on this earth.

Obituary

William Bond Hoover
born to us 5/11/93 9:02 AM
born to heaven 9/14/05 4:29 AM

Beloved son, brother, grandson, nephew, cousin, and friend.
Loved and missed by his parents, Brad and Michelle, and sister, Aubrey.

Memorial service will be Saturday, Sept. 17, 3:00 pm,
at Holy Family Catholic Church. Visitation there from 1-3 pm.

In lieu of flowers, the family respectfully asks that contributions be made to St. Jude Children's Hospital.

Romans 8:38-39

Chapter 8

Left Behind

Wings

"....Fly on, fly on,
Fly on my friend
Go on
Live again"

"Life Without You" by Stevie Ray Vaughan

Liam's final hours were as peaceful as a summer sprinkle of rain. Our wish was that he be comfortable and not be afraid. It was granted.

As most of you know, Liam's original brain tumor resurfaced sometime in mid-August. By the time it declared itself with his seizures (8/31), the spread was quite diffuse throughout the meningeal covering of his brain. Penetration into the brain itself was then a matter of (very short) time. He had not even recovered from his last round of intense chemotherapy when the spread was diagnosed, essentially eliminating any hope of even palliative treatment. Eligibility for any type of clinical trial was out of the question.

Thankfully enough, he did not experience much pain over the last two weeks. His symptoms were mostly limited to fairly intense intermittent vertigo and drowsiness. The latter was also secondary to the fact that he did not sleep very well at night. On his last full day (9/13), he awoke in a general state of confusion. We got him to the hospital, where he was given sedation. The word got out quickly, and we decided to open the door and our hearts to friends and family who could come. School associates and faculty, neighbors, Brad's co-workers, and local family members came and joined us in an all-day vigil. Many were so enriched by the opportunity to bid goodbye to their friend, as were we. Liam never regained consciousness during it all, but I am certain he knew of the countless visitors we had over the course of the day.

Later that night, he lapsed into a deeper rest (coma), and his breathing became slower. About 4 a.m., I stirred when Michelle, who had been laying beside her son for one last night, summoned me. We had a chance to say our goodbyes, with Michelle eloquently telling him that "Jesus is reaching out for you Liam. It's all right to take his hand. Mom and Dad and Aubrey will be ok." I had no such offering, only tears and kisses. At 4:29 he became our Saint Liam. We lay with him for a few minutes, before I walked down the hall to where two of the BA faculty members had made their beds on the floor and chairs that night. I just held Ms. Brasher's hand and said "he's gone", and we walked into the room where she profusely thanked Liam for the chance to know him.

Aubrey has astounded us, her teachers at school and at her religious education class with her articulate manner of describing her feelings. She insisted to us that she be at school that day, mentioning that "my teacher and my classmates will help me through." And they did, making her cards with words of wisdom I could only dream of in the 3rd grade. Aubrey told her classes "I wish I could have spent more time with my brother." In the next breath, she added "but I won't miss him bossing me around." Always did speak what's on her mind. She is our ground support, for sure.

Nevertheless, the pain defies definition. The first few days were spent preparing for his final "celebration" of life, which was magnificent to witness for all. Now, we pick up the pieces of our lives and try and see how and where they fit for our future. As we begin the healing, we know we will always carry a hole in our souls for the son that God needed back in heaven.

It will be filled when we join him again.

"...Life without you
All the love you passed my way
The angels have waited for so long
Now they have their way
Take your place..."

"A Mother's Memorial"

Rejoice in the Lord always. I will say it again, rejoice. The Lord is near. Phil 4:4

It is hard to imagine rejoicing today, but we do. We rejoice in the comfort of knowing that Liam is in the arms of his merciful and compassionate Lord. We take comfort in knowing that in heaven, there is no suffering. There is no pain. There is no cancer, no medicines to choke down, no shots and countless scans to endure. Liam is at peace in the most beautiful place.

Some have said, I prayed so hard for a miracle but it did not come. After three days of reflection, I recall miraculous acts of kindness and validation of the Body of Christ. Over the last fourteen months, I have witnessed compassion beyond my expectations. Children my son's age have amazed me with their honesty, unconditional love and encouragement for Liam. Students who traveled many miles to visit him, ran a marathon in his honor, who have sent cards and letters by the hundreds, who have held lemonade stands and car washes to show their support. Friends have prepared meals, mowed lawns, and sustained us with words of encouragement. Every email is etched in my mind and on my heart. I watched as Liam grew from a shy and easily intimidated boy, to a boy who came to realize his own transformation before he passed. He knew he had become more courageous and brave as he endured his trial. I am thankful that a teacher had him memorize Psalm 23 in his 6th grade year. We recited that Psalm many times in the last few weeks as we lay together at night.

To endure such a loss is gut wrenching. As parents we will learn to assimilate the grief and carry on. Liam would not accept less than that.

"A sword will pierce your own soul too," were words a mother heard. Our heavenly Mother, Mary. Mary endured the death of her son and set an example for all mothers of what to believe and how to live by virtue, faith and hope. My stability comes from the peace and presence of God, our holy mother, and my little saint.

As I look out to each of you, I am honored and proud as his mother, that Liam touched people in some manner. If we have encouraged people in their faith, set an example in some small way, then Liam fulfilled his destiny.

Many people ask, "what can I do for you"? There are two things: whenever you think of Liam, may that memory warm your heart so that he is never forgotten.

Secondly, so that his struggle was not in vain, anytime you have the opportunity to support pediatric cancer research, I beg you to do so. St. Jude depends on donations to continue their research. Vanderbilt, where Liam spent his last few weeks needs your support as well. We have to rid future generations of this disease.

A miracle has taken place; look at the number of people assembled in this house of the Lord, moved by a mighty spirit in the form of a small boy. Thank you for loving my son.

> *Words of Remembrance: spoken by a mother (Michelle Hoover) to her son (Liam Hoover) at his memorial service. September 17, 2005.*

Liam's ceremony was held at the church where we attended and he frequently altar-served, and over 900 people were in attendance. Michelle and I now realize we had this protective "fog" that descended around us in those first hours and days after Liam's passing, and we used this insulation to focus on the specifics of the service. Outstanding music, moving testimony, and superb coordination and direction were the order of the day and carried out with aplomb by a handful of our Christian brethren. Every word, spoken and sung, was treasured and so very pertinent. It was a **celebration**, mixed with tears and some spontaneous laughter as Liam's life and times were recounted. So many persons related to us that they had never been witness to such a life-defining event, and so profoundly moved.

One vignette from the service: I had recounted the story of Liam's and my "word play" game, when I would call out a word and he would say the first thing that popped into his head. I had said "beautiful" and he said "Mom", but since he had already given that pat answer to my previous word "pretty" I asked him to think of another. He then replied "the golf coach at BA. That's what the guys told me." I sort of nodded to the section of the sanctuary where his class was seated and they all chuckled. Later though, one of Liam's favorite teachers came to the podium to share some memories, and he brought the house down when he introduced himself:

"Hello", he began, "I'm the golf coach from BA".

Aftermath

"All my world...all I've lost.
Your hand restores
Your works make whole...
You're all that it means to live"

"Devotion" by Newsboys

Michelle, Aubrey, and I are marking unique moments of praise and celebration. One such event occurred on October 1 at a Newsboys concert. Having purchased tickets the day they went on sale back in July, we had planned for the four of us to enjoy the show. Liam had 3-4 of their CD's (the most of any artists in his collection), and was looking quite forward to seeing them live again. Friends of ours had arranged for us to meet the band backstage. After Liam passed, we decided we would still go and celebrate his life in song. We met the lead singer (Peter Furler), who was speechless at our story and said as much. I told him that words were not necessary, but that his music spoke for him. He replied "that means so much to us; it makes what we do worthwhile." I then asked about a particular song, that I didn't know if it was in the set list for that evening, but it was Liam's favorite. "If it's not," he said, "we'll put it there." We thanked him for his time, and then a staffer escorted us to the merchandise table. We were given each a T-shirt, and they gave Michelle and I a CD and DVD, and wristbands for the girls.

By that time, the opening band was almost done with their set. We got to our seats (third row) just as they struck up their closing song "Beautiful One". Liam loved this song, and it was played as an accompaniment to the slideshow at the service. We all blinked back tears. The following two bands came and went, and then it was time for the headliner Newsboys. After the opening song, the lead singer said "I know some of you are hurting out there, are carrying burdens..." I looked over to Michelle and Aubrey, who were clutching each other. He continued, "And this is for Liam" as the band launched into Million Pieces. Simultaneously, confetti rained down from above the stage as they played, and we were awash in smiles and tears (and paper). The band could see us and nodded a time or two, as we flashed them a thumbs-up sign. The remainder of the concert was a blur, as we enjoyed song after song. We know Liam did too.

Later that week, Michelle and I were invited to lunch at Liam's middle school. It was "Liam Hoover bandanna day", with every student, teacher, and cafeteria employee sporting bandannas. We were announced as guests, and the entire student body came to their feet for an ovation. It was mutually uplifting, as we were told how inspired his classmates are to see us functioning. They and so many more mourn with us, and are processing the loss of their friend and classmate in their own particular ways.

We have occasions on the calendar that will keep us looking forward. The St. Jude Marathon promises to be a memorable time. And, there is a 5K race locally that some friends are putting together (for St. Jude) in November. Anticipating these events help to offset the heartaches, such as Michelle composing a letter to Liam's sponsored pen-pal in Mexico, Victoriano, explaining why Liam won't be writing him again. Or walking by the shoe rack in the garage past his favorite, and almost new, Birkenstocks. Closing a college account that he will never get to use.

Grieving well. That just about describes us. Well, in body and spirit, and of course, missing our boy. The absolute shock is ebbing, day by day, yet it is still so unreal. Surreal. Yet, we are sustained by Hope. No, not our new kitten (named Hope), obtained sans my permission while out of town last week! She has, as Michelle put it, brought a smile or two to our faces. But the deeper Hope to which I am referring is in waiting "in joyful <u>hope</u> in the coming of our Lord..." - Romans 12:12

Day by day, hour by hour, minute by minute. That's how one goes on after tragedy. And you hold on together. Although intuitive to me, I wrote Michelle a card the week or so after the service stating that I would never give up on our union, that I would be right here beside her through any- and everything to come. In my mind, that is paramount to survival. I would simply shut the negative thoughts from my consciousness, every Satan-placed rumination of getting away from this life and starting over, etc. I can see how one might choose this path, because I can see how it might be perceived as the easy way out. But it is not what we promised to each other, before God, in 1989. It would also have been tempting for us to draw the curtains and shut out the world indefinitely, and for a time that was necessary for our own sanity, but over time we opened up the curtain to let others who were waiting to uplift us do just that. We could not fathom how much love and support was to come.

Void

When you are going through hell, keep going.
Winston Churchill

Oddly enough, we feel the profoundness of our loss more deeply now than in the immediate time after 9/14/05. Not unusual, we have read, to be insulated from the initial sense of grief while taking care of the requisite business in those first few days and weeks. Now, we are left only with the daily reality of life without our son. We continue to of course realize what we have relayed before, that he is at peace and with Jesus, and that there will be a joyful reunion someday. But "someday" seems a very long time from now.

Cards and letters continue to pour in, along with donations to St. Jude (now well over $32,000!). Michelle's birthday was this week, and we were able to get away for a couple of days to San Francisco (last minute change from a Wilma-cancelled trip to the Cancun area). Friends of hers got her a very nice "circle of life" necklace, consisting of a diamond-rimmed pendant of Liam's birthstone (emerald). The jeweler assisting them with the purchase related his loss of a child, and fashioned the meaningful design. He suggested that instead of a birthday gift, attaching a Biblical time significance to it such as 40 days after Liam's passage into heaven. 40 days, a recurring theme in the Bible, to include the interval between Jesus' resurrection and ascension, seemed appropriate. And 40 days after Liam's passing was....Michelle's birthday. And her 40th, of course (she okayed this revelation).

While in the Bay area, we had a chance to take a walk through a nearby Redwood forest (Muir Woods). It was a peaceful day, and we were enjoying the beauty of God's creation together. Michelle, unbeknownst to me, had been communing with Liam and asked him to send a sign, any sign, that he was there with us. At that moment, I pointed out to her a small pile of animal refuse and wondered what wild critter may have left us that. She chuckled, relating her wish to Liam and, taking this as his "sign", and said she was glad he still had his sense of humor.

Liam lives on, and yet another sign of that is the "Hoover Run for Hope", a 5K route that is scheduled for November 19 (see prior email). We continue to anticipate, and train for, the St. Jude run in December. We may have as many as 100 runners on the "Team Liam" for that event. Heroes, every one of them.

Halloween has come and gone, and with it a fresh reminder of our void. We know upcoming holidays will bring a similar sting, but we will not let it negatively impact Aubrey. She by the way brought home straight A's on her report card, a first for her!

"Everybody hurts...sometimes." as REM put it in 1993 (ironically, the year of Liam's birth). We realize that so many hurt with us, and are going through their personal journey of pain and acceptance. "Take comfort in your friends." We must continue to take comfort in one another, and embody the spirit of Liam, who was sent here "to spread love" (as per his bookmark). He would want nothing less. Tragedy and hardship knows no bounds, and does not take a break. Just this week a friend of mine from the Army found out his wife has a brain tumor. Our hearts ache anew. We have learned from you how to offer warmth in times of crises; now we put it to use.

"You are not alone...so hold on."

Friends of ours put together a local 5K run in memory of Liam, and the inaugural "Hoover Run For Hope" was a rousing success:

"And the King will answer and say to them, 'Assuredly, I say to you, inasmuch as you did *it* to one of the least of these My brethren, you did *it* to Me.'" Matthew 25:40

We witnessed over 650 men, women and children doing it for Him with their feet on Saturday (11/19/05) at the inaugural Hoover Run For Hope. This 5K event, and 1 mile kids' run, which started and finished at Kenrose Elementary School and wound through the neighborhoods where our son Liam grew and played, was a memorable occasion for all present. Over $29,000 was raised for the patients and families of St. Jude Children's Research Hospital. This institution, founded by Danny Thomas in 1962, is not only a pioneer in children's cancer research but provides its services to patients and families at no out-of-pocket cost. Moreover, transportation to and from the hospital is reimbursed, there is a daily food allowance, and there are three separate free housing facilities for families while their children are in Memphis receiving treatment. Events such as our race are conducted all over the country and beyond to support the daily St. Jude operational expenditure of just under 1 million dollars.

Pulling the event together in six weeks was a gargantuan task, and was done by a bevy of volunteers from Liam's former elementary school and his middle school. Generous corporate sponsors provided commemorative T-shirts, drinks and refreshments, and website and brochure generation. Heartfelt appreciation is extended to all involved in the remarkable success of the day.

Our son Liam is profoundly missed by many, and we feel his absence daily. We continue though to be uplifted by the body of Christ, manifested through all who came together to make the *Hoover Run for Hope* a reality. In two weeks, we anticipate another joyous celebration at the St. Jude Marathon, where over 100 runners from our area will converge in Memphis to raise additional funds for St. Jude. Liam's legacy continues: a spirit of hope for children with cancer.

I told people that it mattered not the amount of dollars raised, and if only $200 was generated it was well worth the time and effort to watch so many come together for a cause. The word "community" never had a better definition.

Two weeks later, about 80 of us from the Nashville area gathered in Memphis for the annual St. Jude Marathon. Some ran the half marathon, and some the 5K event, and all experienced an overwhelming feeling of accomplishment for the patients and families of St. Jude, present and future. About 40 members from the hospital staff where I work, engineered by the CEO, came down and participated as well. This was commemorated by the state representative in that district with a proclamation commending "Team Liam", signed by the Governor. All of all wore our "Team Liam" shirts, garnering numerous pats-on-the-back and shouts of encouragement along the way. My neighbor, an accomplished distance runner, told me that he was passed by a woman who, after seeing Liam's picture and the message beneath the picture for several miles as she trailed him, told him she was about to be overcome with emotion. "So she dropped me!" he said, a little miffed at the prospect. It was equally bittersweet and inspirational for Michelle and me during the run, passing by places where we spent many of our last days, weeks and months with our son. But run we did, and finished, with sweat and tears along the way.

Chapter 9

Remembrances

I explained to our friends and family that we would not be sending traditional Christmas cards out this year. Instead, I shared with them a few of the poignant messages we had received over the past 18 months, culled from all the cards, emails, and even a phone conversation we had with a priest from our former parish. A teacher from BA collected acrostic descriptions of Liam which were compiled into the following card:

Christmas 2005

"And I saw Liaaaaaaaam running playing tag with his sister oh yeah
I saw him swimming and splashing and he had no pain, he had no pain"
  "No Pain" composed by a 6th grader neighborhood pal (complete lyrics below)

"Dear Aubrey, you are always smiling and you make me smile too. Tell Liam I said hi and I'm looking out for you while he is gone."
  Stephen, age 7 (10/04)

"Liam...precious child – yours, and His – <u>still</u> in his loving care..."
  Colleague of Brad's

"Always smiling...my hero...too cool for words...a brother in Christ...a good friend...part of us always...inspirational...funny...a regular boy...role model... beyond words..."
  Various friends

Loved his family, friends, and being at BA

Is always a part of the Class of 2011

Always had a smile on his face and a kind word for others

More than happy to praise God

Hero to everyone—instead of a cape, he wore a bandana!

Overall, he wanted to be just a regular boy

Oh! What a great person he was!

Very fun to hang around with

Excited to come to school with his teachers and friends

Responsible student who always had his work in on time

Born to us: May 11, 1993 *Born to heaven:* September 14, 2005
The Lord is my shepherd; I shall not want. (Ps. 23:1)

"…Until we all link back up at the ultimate rally point, God's speed to you and your little soldier…"

Army buddy who served with Brad in Germany and Desert Storm

"Many times your influence will be in ways that won't look to the world as impressive as that big check [from the Hoover Run for Hope]; but will be equally important, as people are impacted by you in quiet places, unknown to you, as you live out your life."

A Brentwood Academy dad

"And this is for Liam."

Peter Furler, lead singer of Newsboys (a contemporary Christian band), dedicating Liam's favorite song "Million Pieces" at their concert October 1 in Nashville

"I hope you all feel God's presence. He's probably never been closer."

A neighbor who experienced great personal loss earlier this year.

"A lifetime gift. That is what Liam gave each one of the class of 2011. Bits of character and lessons of love and empathy that came from Liam and were left with each of our children. Many years from now, maybe you will hear stories of some of these children, grown into adulthood, who are performing acts of unselfish service. Perhaps one will be a doctor searching for a cure for cancer, who remembers these last 14 months that were by that time many years ago. Maybe one will be a teacher, who takes that extra minute to utter a caring word to a hurting child. Whatever they are doing, I hope you grin from ear to ear knowing that your precious one helped shape the men and women they have become.

Remember those little faces: the girls who loved on Liam and doted on him like little mothers when you weren't there. And the boys who let him just be Liam, but at the same time watched protectively over him like brothers. See your son in each of their faces, because he is there.

A Brentwood Academy mother

"...Aubrey may grow up to be the kindest, most thoughtful partner a man could ever love. You have a great wife. You've been a real man. A dad. Liam was a blessing for all of you."

Med school classmate of Brad's

"...We love the One who called Liam home. He has the prior claim."

An 89 year-old senior citizen friend of the family

"When times get hard...I will ask myself 'how would Liam take this on?' Then I too will succeed."

A BA classmate of Liam's

"...at the cross-country meet I ran in honor...of Liam. My goal that day was to run my personal best and armed with the inspiration of your son's fight...I achieved that goal, as well as running one of the fastest times in BA's history on that course. Today I would like to give you the medal I received in your son's honor. I hope this will be a reminder for you of the prize for which God called Liam."

A BA 8th grader

"Liam was one of those patients that could make us smile just knowing he was inpatient."

St. Jude nurse

"You offered Liam his only chance at being cured...future patients will benefit from his participation in the clinical trials at St. Jude."

One of Liam's St. Jude physicians

"The memorial service...was the culmination of [my religious journey]. I finally got it that Saturday (FAITH) and I have your family, and Liam, to thank for that."

Fellow Holy Family parishioner

"Jesus will see to it that Liam is not afraid. And, when they are together, Liam and Jesus will see to it that you aren't either."

Father Liam (priest from San Antonio)

"Lili – save me a spot up there."
Message on a wooden cross given to us by Liam's friends

"I get the spot after Chris."
Same source

My First Christmas in Heaven

I see the countless Christmas trees around the world below,
with tiny lights like heavens stars reflecting on the snow.
The sight is so spectacular! Please wipe away the tears,
for I am spending Christmas with Jesus Christ this year.
I hear the many Christmas songs that people hold so dear,
but the sound of music can't compare with the Christmas choir up here.
I have no words to tell you the joy their faces bring,
for it is beyond description to hear the angels sing.
I know how much you miss me; I see the pain inside your heart.
But I am not really far away; we really aren't apart.

So be happy for me dear ones you know I hold you dear,
for I am spending Christmas with Jesus Christ this year.
I send you a special gift from the heavenly home above,
I send you each a memory of my undying love.
After all, love is a gift more precious than pure gold.
It was always most important in the stories Jesus told.
Please love and keep each other as my Father said to do,
for I can't count the blessings or love he has for you.

So have a Merry Christmas with Jesus Christ this year.
Liam Hoover (via an online support group post)

Additional Messages:
"When I first moved he Liam told me "if you need any help I'm here" and now he's not. I'm so sad."
Elementary school chum

"Liam your spirit will always be in my heart. Goodness will come out of this situation."
From a classmate who recently lost her father to cancer

"Down through the years there have been certain names that need no last name to identify them: Elvis, Cher, etc. Now, we have Liam."

6th grade teacher of Liam's

"I hate cancer with all of my heart. It has taken away my grandmother and now my hero."

BA classmate

"See ya Liam".

Anonymous

"No Pain" (Liam's Song)
CJ Wochomurka 11/02/05

I came home one Wednesday afternoon
Saw my parents all full of gloom
I asked my mom what was wrong
But all she said was that he was gone
That night I prayed to God
Asking why he was gone
I wondered why he had left
But that night when I slept...

Chorus:
I saw Liaaaaaaaam running playing tag with his sister, oh yeah
I saw him swimming and splashing and he had no pain, he had no pain

I woke up the very next day
Went to a flagpole to be silent and pray
I asked his mom if she was ok
She said I'm fine he's in a better place
I said God loves him, she said I know
I just wish he didn't have to go

Repeat chorus

Oh Liam why did you have to go
We all love you and miss you so
I really miss you but don't we all
You and your bandana standing bright and tall

We're getting over Liam's death
But all miss him no doubt about that
Sometimes I cry sometimes I'm happy
But I don't mean to get all sappy
I just want you to have one more thing to hear
And that's that Liam had no fear

And I saw Liam running playing tag with his sister oh yeah
I saw him swimming and splashing and he had no pain, he had noooo paiiiiiiiinnn

Postscript

Blessed are they that mourn, for they shall be comforted. Matthew 5:4

Four months after Liam's passing, we have not experienced "comfort" in the literal sense. I do not believe we will appreciate the reality of this beatitude until we are joined again in reunion with our son. Our entire lives, and the very way we view every aspect of life, is irreversibly altered. The acuteness of the absolute hurt will (and has, to a degree) diminished, but the absence and its effects are chronic.

Yet, we do find vestiges of reassurance. Liam's entire class hand-wrote me birthday messages in January (and did the same for Michelle last October). "Dear Dr. Hoover", one began, "I have never been able to forget our trip to Memphis last year when we visited Liam. It was one of the best days of my life." Another one related "I was in Liam's Bible class last year, and I was there when he asked Christ into his heart." The best birthday gift I could have asked for; Liam never related that event.

The goodness in people continues to manifest itself, almost daily. A St. Jude home being built now for donation via raffle this summer will be done so in Liam's name. Aubrey's softball league will honor her brother's memory with their annual charity event this spring. We continue to receive tribute notations to St. Jude in his memory weekly. It is so very apparent that we are not alone in our sorrow. The loss of our son has affected humanity, both those we know firsthand and those impacted by the rippling effect of his, and our, story. John Donne put it best when he penned that "no man is an island; entire of itself; every man is a piece of the continent, a part of the main." "...any man's death diminishes me, because I am involved in mankind, and therefore never send to know for whom the bells tolls; it tolls for thee."

I share with you the following, found on a website dedicated to a 5 year-old boy with neuroblastoma, who shared Liam's name, and joined him in heaven last November:

The Brave Little Soul
by John Alessi

Not too long ago in Heaven there was a little soul who took wonder in observing the world. He especially enjoyed the love he saw there and often expressed this joy with God. One day however the little soul was sad, for on this day he saw suffering in the world. He approached God and sadly asked, "Why do bad things happen; why is there suffering in the world?"

God paused for a moment and replied, "Little soul, do not be sad, for the suffering you see, unlocks the love in people's hearts." The little soul was confused. "What do you mean," he asked." God replied, "Have you not noticed the goodness and love that is the offspring of that suffering? Look at how people come together, drop their differences and show their love and compassion for those who suffer. All their other motivations disappear and they become motivated by love alone."

The little soul began to understand and listened attentively as God continued, "The suffering soul unlocks the love in people's hearts much like the sun and the rain unlock the flower within the seed. I created everyone with endless love in their heart, but unfortunately most people keep it locked up and hardly share it with anyone. They are afraid to let their love shine freely, because they are afraid of being hurt. But a suffering soul unlocks that love. I tell you this - it is the greatest miracle of all. Many souls have bravely chosen to go into the world and suffer - to unlock this love – to create this miracle - for the good of all humanity."

Just then the little soul got a wonderful idea and could hardly contain himself. With his wings fluttering, bouncing up and down, the little soul excitedly replied, "I am brave; let me go! I would like to go into the world and suffer so that I can unlock the goodness and love in people's hearts! I want to create that miracle!"

God smiled and said, "You are a brave soul I know, and thus I will grant your request. But even though you are very brave you will not be able to do this alone. I have known since the beginning of time that you would ask for this and so I have carefully selected many souls to care for you on your journey. Those souls will help you create your miracle; however they will also share in your suffering. Two of these souls are most special and will care for you, help you and suffer along with you, far beyond the others. They have already chosen a name for you."

God and the brave little soul shared a smile, and then embraced. In parting, God said, "Do not forget little soul that I will be with you always. Although you have agreed to bear the pain, you will do so through my strength. And if the time should come when you feel that you have suffered enough, just say the word, think the thought, and you will be healed."

Thus at that moment the brave little soul was born into the world, and through his suffering and God's strength, he unlocked the goodness and love in people's hearts. For so many people dropped their differences and came together to show their love. Priorities became properly aligned. People gave from their hearts. Those that were always too busy found time. Many began new spiritual journeys – some regained lost faith – many came back to God. Parents hugged their children tighter. Friends and family grew closer. Old friends got together and new friendships were made. Distant family reunited, and every family spent more time together. Everyone prayed. Peace and love reigned. Lives changed forever. It was good. The world was a better place. The miracle had happened. God was pleased.

Quotes, song verses, Scripture...Michelle and I have found meaning in each. But we will never fully understand some things on this earth. We do take some solace in the fact that we have no regrets regarding the decisions we made with the treatment of Liam from the beginning, and similarly hold no anger whatsoever at the caregivers who did all they could for our son at each turn and bend. Yes, the sadness is still overwhelming, and it will sneak up on us and grab us when we are not "expecting" it. New Year's Eve was a sucker punch, with Aubrey gone visiting relatives in Texas and Michelle and I home alone. Deafening quiet it was, and what exactly did we have to look forward to in 2006? I will hear a song on the radio that the DJ remarked debuted 30 years ago ("More Than A Feeling" by Boston for you classic rockers), and I shudder to think of how long I must wait to see my son again (given that I reach the average lifespan). Until then, I will continue to reflect and ponder.

And remember.

"I just want to remind you that I love you."

Cell phone message left for me by Liam in July 2003.

Archived forever.

Chapter 10

"A Time to Heal"

Encore

"A time to heal." One of the most touching observations offered to me was from my friend who asked me how Michelle and I were coping and getting along. I told him I felt we had grown closer through it all and he agreed, saying "I have seen that too." Only two people in this entire world know precisely the pain we have endured, and she and I will continue our walk together. Forever. Stronger.

Though not what we'd envisioned to do, we have become quite the fund-raisers. We recently topped the $100,000 mark with St. Jude donations in Liam's memory, which will garner us a plaque displayed somewhere in the new six-story wing that is currently under construction on the SJCH campus. It won't be in the main lobby though, since that requires a $10 million donation to get a plaque there! We are honored that a local builder has dedicated a St. Jude dream home giveaway in memory of Liam. The home will feature a plaque with Liam's picture with that winsome smile of his and will be given to a lucky $100 raffle ticket buyer.

We also just wrapped up a successful fundraising event for the Neuro-Oncology Division at Vanderbilt Children's Hospital, again in Liam's name. Aubrey's softball league sponsored a songwriter's night concert that was a magical evening for all in attendance. The night was kicked off by an outstanding three-song set by a choral ensemble (the Academy Juniors) from Liam's middle school, Brentwood Academy. Chris Sanders, formerly of the Tennessee Titans, was on-hand and delivered poignant remarks. We garnered items for a silent auction from artists such as Brad Paisley, the Newsboys, and George Jones, just to name a few. We topped out over $20,000 in total collections and proceeds.

I prepared some remarks regarding the support and love that Aubrey's team gave to her during Liam's relapse, and have taken the liberty to include that below for those interested. Before she and I took the stage, the emcee for the event (a local DJ for a popular Nashville radio station) offered a few remarks. "I do not know the Hoover family or their story," he began, "but I do know how great an institution that Vanderbilt Children's Hospital is to so many children, etc." After my presentation, accompanied by our friend Jeff from church on piano as he did at the memorial service along with the slideshow of Liam, the emcee could just utter "Wow" and shake his head.

The entertainment? Songwriters of hits by the likes of Brad Paisley and Joe Nichols, for starters. Ken Harrell's "You Restore My Soul" was a highlight, and Tim Nichols' "Live Like You Were Dying" brought the house down. Liam's physician from Vanderbilt was there sitting beside us, and those who were able to make it witnessed a wonderful evening of love, exhilaration, and yes, hope. To top things off, we held a live auction of the four barstools that the songwriters sat upon during the show. These stools were painted by Michelle, with help from 3 patients from Vanderbilt Children's Hospital, and garnered about $4500 total at auction. One of the buyers, a coach and board member of the league, then came to the front and called Aubrey up there with him. He presented the barstool to her as a gift, much to our utter astonishment. It sits proudly in her room.

Someone asked me not long ago what days in the coming weeks and months do I "dread" in regards to Liam not being here? Tough question, and though his birthday and Mother's Day come to mind, we know that any day may bring a sting. We have found for example Saturdays to be especially hard, and particularly empty at times. Yet, each day holds another dear memory to be reflected upon, be it with a smile, or tear, or both.

And brings us one day closer.

Worry does not empty tomorrow of sorrows; it empties today of strength
Corrie Ten Boom

Songwriter's Night Benefit/Auction
Remarks by the author
04/21/06

Good evening and welcome. I would like to welcome our Life Teen Music Director Jeff Thomas, who will accompany these remarks and the slide-show with a piano rendition of Liam's favorite song, "Beautiful One" as he did at Liam's memorial service 7 months ago. He will then perform an additional song.

Ronnie Swayze approached me last December with the suggestion that EWA select our family as the designee for the benefit event this spring, in memory of Liam. Michelle and I were of course honored by this gesture, and immediately chose Vanderbilt Children's Hospital to be the beneficiary of the concert proceeds. As some or most of you know, Liam underwent the majority of his treatment at St. Jude. After his relapse in June of last year, we wanted to stay closer to home and Vanderbilt, in close contact with SJ, provided excellent care for us right up to the end last September.

I would like to share a story with you and demonstrate what a team of Lil Squealers, and later the Blue Tigers, now the Red Devils, meant to a nine-year-old girl who experienced a trauma no child should.

On the last full day for Liam on this earth, we had to take him into the hospital for some much-needed sedation. My sister-in-law picked up Aubrey from school and brought her to the hospital room where we were. Now, Aubrey had seen Liam in such an environment many times, and walked into the room asking "what's up" as she glanced over at Liam resting. I am sure she just figured he was napping, as she had seen him do all too often of late. I sat Aubrey on my lap, and recounted to her what we had talked about just last night as she was going to bed.

"What's the worst thing a person can get?" she had asked. I thought for a moment and told her heart disease. She asked, "Do people die of heart disease?" "Sometimes," I answered. "How about cancer," she persisted, "do people die of that too?" "Sometimes," was my reply again. "Is Liam going to die?" was the question I knew was next. "Well, I hope not, but if God decides to take him that's what may happen," I answered rather quickly. "Oh, I hope not" was her reply before going off to sleep.

"Remember what I said last night about how sometimes people die of cancer, or heart disease?" She began to nod slowly. "Well," nodding at her brother,"God has decided to take Liam home with him." I barely got out before she dissolved into tears and sobs. It was a heartbreaking moment of course, and she went over and hugged her brother. (I think I saw him scowl just a bit as she did...no lie...if anything could get a rise out of him, it was her). Her first fall league softball games were that very evening, a doubleheader, and she had been anticipating it so much. "I don't think I want to go to my game," she said, through her tears. I told her that was fine and she could stay here with us or go home with her cousins. A bit later, she came back with "Well, maybe I could go to the second game and just watch." I told her again that would be ok – whatever she felt like doing. Finally, she stated "I think I will go and play the games. My teammates will help me through." And they did, with an opening prayer prior to the game that I wish I could have heard, and continual support and hugs throughout both games, and the season.

Aubrey had never played any competitive team sport before signing on with the Lil Squealers in the spring of 2005. From the start, Coach Carrie was as much concerned with the game of life and fostering relationships as she was with grounders and hitting the ball (though you wouldn't know it by listening to her at practice!). She saw to it that Aubrey blended right in with the team, and they with her, and when she found out about Liam's illness she insisted that when he was well enough – he would be the ball boy. He is, Carrie, he is.

Coach Lori continued this sense of teamwork with the team, made up of essentially the same girls, in the fall. Aubrey will never remember the won-loss record, but will never forget the support and love a bunch of 8-9 year olds gave to her. And through her, to us.

For these life skills that you Carrie and Lori, and all of the EWA staff and coaches, have taught and instilled, not to mention all of you wonderful parents; we tip our caps to you. God Bless.

We met with a group of nurses from Vanderbilt involved in a research project centered around families who have suffered the loss of a child (or sibling). We agreed to participate and to share our experience. During the one-on-one interview, I was asked what advice or insight I might want to share with others encountering this sort of loss. I offered that any loss is unique to itself, be it the loss of any family member, to divorce and/or separation, to the unforeseen end of a chosen career, etc. Even within the confines of the loss of a child, I am not at liberty to fully empathize with any other family given the vicissitudes of each situation.

However, I continued, I can only relate how we have "managed to manage" as I have put it. For starters, all the "advice" we read about not making any major life decisions for at least one year after the loss – poppycock! We set that one on its ear by following our hearts and minds in deciding to relocate (about 4 miles away, building our first – and hopefully, last – home). We have also moved ahead with expanding our family, hoping and praying for the miracle of adoption again. And we made these decisions within 4 months of Liam's passing, with no regrets and no turning back. As we have come to fully realize, the Holy Spirit is our guide. And we follow.

Epilogue

In His Own Words

I feel that I am most like the character Bilbo Baggins from The Hobbit. I learned from reading The Hobbit that Bilbo and I are similar in appearance and in our character.

I am short in height like Bilbo. He and I like adventures. Like Bilbo, I miss my home if I am gone for too long. Furthermore, I think Bilbo and me (sic) are alike in the way we are strong. Bilbo learned that he was strong after saving the dwarves many times. Before I got cancer I did not think I was very brave. I think I am brave and stronger because of all I have been through.

I am similar to Bilbo in many ways.

Liam Hoover 09/05
Last writing assignment

Afterword

August 18, 2014

This year marks a decade since Liam's diagnosis, and also the year that his story and ours will find its way into print. So much has occurred of course since 2004, both encouraging and discouraging, not unlike anyone blessed with life on this earth. We did adopt another son in 2007, aptly named Gabriel (loosely translated as "man of God"). Aubrey is now a senior in high school, both beautiful and enigmatic as ever.

We speak of Liam often, and young Gabriel is quite inquisitive and we are pleased to answer his questions. Not that we concur with his logic sometimes. One day, while driving home from somewhere, he asks "Daddy - heaven is wonderful right?"

"Right," I reply.

"And Liam is there having fun right?"

"Right" I repeat.

"And you have to die to get there right?"

"Right" for the third time, thinking this is the charm and he'll move on.

"Well," he says, "I want to be dead. So I can play with Liam."

If any of you could fashion a quick response to that, let me know since I could not.

As I write this final chapter in this book, we are preparing for a relocation to Florida. We anticipate new adventures and building fresh relationships in the Sunshine State, and hearing the Gulf break against the shore and the calm it brings. We will consider another element in closure, in the physical realm, with Liam by perhaps a burial (scattering) at sea. Yet, as with all that has transpired since his passing, we believe we will know when the time is right.

As always.

"...And a little child shall lead them." Is 11:6

CPSIA information can be obtained at www.ICGtesting.com
Printed in the USA
LVOW10s0311310315

432669LV00001B/158/P